Warrior · 82

Osprey

US Submarine Crewman 1941–45

Robert Hargis · Illustrated by Velimir Vuksic

First published in Great Britain in 2003 by Osprey Publishing,
Elms Court, Chapel Way, Botley, Oxford OX2 9LP, UK.
Email: info@ospreypublishing.com

A CIP catalog record for this book is available from the British Library

ISBN 1 84176 588 0

Robert Hargis has asserted his/her right under the Copyright, Designs and
Patents Act, 1988, to be identified as the Author of this Work

Editor: Gerard Barker
Design: Ken Vail Graphic Design, Cambridge, UK
Index by Bob Munro

Originated by Grasmere Digital Imaging, Leeds, UK
Printed in China through World Print Ltd.

03 04 05 06 07   10 9 8 7 6 5 4 3 2 1

FOR A CATALOG OF ALL BOOKS PUBLISHED BY OSPREY MILITARY AND
AVIATION PLEASE CONTACT:

Osprey Direct USA, c/o MBI Publishing, P.O. Box 1,
729 Prospect Ave, Osceola, WI 54020, USA
E-mail: info@ospreydirectusa.com

Osprey Direct UK, P.O. Box 140, Wellingborough, Northants, NN8 2FA, UK
E-mail: info@ospreydirect.co.uk

www.ospreypublishing.com

Artist's note

Readers may care to note that the original paintings from
which the color plates in this book were prepared are
available for private sale. All reproduction copyright
whatsoever is retained by the Publishers. All enquiries
should be addressed to:

Velimir Vuksic
Ilica 54
Zagreb
1000
Croatia

The Publishers regret that they can enter into no
correspondence upon this matter.

Acknowledgements

The author would like to dedicate this book to all US Navy
Submarine Sailors and especially to those of the 52 boats
on 'Eternal Patrol'. Special thanks to the US Submarine
Veterans Association for their assistance in locating
submarine veterans to help in the preparation of this book.
Last but not least the following veterans who made specific
contributions to the book with their stories must be
thanked: Billy A. Grieves, John Close, Theodore Breisch,
Kenneth M. Jones, Richard B. Fason, James H. Hintzman,
Ron 'Warshot' Smith and Victor M. Radwick.

FRONT COVER **While not often used during the War due to
the fact that submarines operated in blackout conditions,
searchlights were standard equipment on all US
submarines. (US Navy Photograph)**

CONTENTS

US SUBMARINE CREWMAN 1941–45

INTRODUCTION

The history of the United States submarine service is both long and eventful. From the earliest use of a submersible in combat, Bushnell's *Turtle*, to the modern-day nuclear-attack submarines of the Los Angeles class, the US Navy has been at the cutting edge of submarine warfare tactics and technology. Nowhere is this more evident than in the efforts of United States submarine crews during World War Two. Long dubbed the 'Silent Service', due to the secret nature of their work, the crews of US Navy submarines conducted a successful undersea campaign during World War Two.

THE STORY OF US SUBMARINES IN WORLD WAR TWO

During World War One German U-boats had been responsible for some of the War's most notable calamities – the sinking of the SS *Lusitania* and SS *Arabic* in 1915 to name but two. Indeed, by squeezing Britain's supply lines to both her domestic population and her army abroad, unrestricted submarine warfare almost won the War for Germany. Eventually the German U-boat menace was overcome and the United States' entry into the War provided the additional men and materials needed by the Allied forces to win the War. The lessons of that War, however, were not lost on the handful of dedicated submarine officers around the world who saw the submarine as a powerful strategic weapon capable of decisive action.

In the years immediately following World War One the US Navy, like many other forces in the world, was in a state of transition. The bloodbath of the 'Great' War had made the public weary of the military and all its applications. Navies around the world began to cut back on their weapon expenditure. The 1920s became an era of disarmament. When at the Washington Naval Conference the United States called for a massive reduction in the world's navies, most nations eagerly grasped the opportunity to reduce their weapons inventory. Submarine warfare, like poison gas and the machine gun, was seen as a symptom of what was wrong in the world. Military journals and newspapers called into question the need for the existence of a weapon that is, by its very nature, stealthy.

Before the start of World War Two there were two primary schools of thought with regard to the use of submarines in the US Navy: the fleet concept and the concept of commerce destruction. The US Navy, with its 'Fleet-in-Being' concept of the big-gun battleship, viewed the submarine in its prewar strategies primarily as a fleet-type weapon to be used much like cavalry in a land army. It would be employed on offensive operations against other naval targets, to protect the fleet from other submarines, and as a scout.

A minority of sailors supported the idea of using submarines against the commerce of other maritime nations, but it was a concept much out of favor with the public and the commanders of the fleet, both of whom saw the tactic as being underhanded. If the submarine could be used against merchant vessels, what would the result be if the same vessels were turned against the battle line? Being the conservative body that they were, officers of the prewar US naval community focused on the development of a submarine to meet the needs of traditional fleet tactics, although, ironically, such a high-speed vessel with its extremely long range of operation would also be highly suitable for commerce raiding. This discussion of tactical doctrine eventually resulted in the development of the US 'fleet boat', like the Gato and Balao class vessels that would be used with such great effectiveness in the Pacific War.

By early 1943 the US Navy was being equipped with the newer Balao class submarines, constructed of stronger high-tensile steel, allowing them to operate at depths of up to 400 feet. (National Archives)

The submarines of the US Navy were constructed at one of four ship or navy yards. The Pacific facility, Mare Island, produced 16 fleet submarines during the War including the famous boats, *Wahoo* and *Tang*. The comparatively small number of boats produced at Mare Island during the War is not due to any inefficiency at the navy yard, but rather to the fact that the facility was primarily devoted to the repair and overhaul of existing boats. In the Midwest, 28 boats were turned out from the Manitowoc Shipyard, Wisconsin and floated down the Mississippi to make their way to war. The East Coast had two large shipyards – Electric Boat Company at Groton, Connecticut and the Portsmouth Navy Yard at Portsmouth, New Hampshire – that together produced 144 submarines during the War.

The Japanese air raid on Pearl Harbor all but destroyed America's main force of battleships in the Pacific, and as result the US Navy was left with few options as to how to attack Japan - one of these was to wage unrestricted submarine warfare on the commerce of the island empire. Thus from late 1941, the primary task for US submarines would be to bring Japan to her knees by cutting her trade and restricting her ability to supply the far-flung forces of her empire. In this US tactics during the first two years of the War were far from satisfactory, with many problems arising both in the area of command and with materials.

The prewar training of submarine commanders had placed emphasis on submerged sonar approaches and attacks. Consequently, commanders who allowed their boats to be detected were often reprimanded for their failure, because in training for war during the 1930s a sighted submarine was considered to be a sunken submarine. It was widely held in the prewar navy that the detonation of 400 pounds of TNT up to 300 feet from a submerged target like a submarine was likely to cause the target irreparable damage. This official disapproval of aggressive tactics that might lead to a submarine being spotted made for a breed of technically superior but rather timid officers. As a consequence, early in the War all attacks on Japanese vessels were conducted in a slow, methodical manner, with submerged sonar approaches that more often than not allowed the enemy to escape.

Another problem with naval submarine tactics lay in three major defects suffered by American torpedoes. At the start of the conflict the newest American submarines were armed with the Bliss-Leavitt Mk. XIV torpedo, equipped with the Mk. VI exploder. The Mk. VI exploder was a device that had both a contact detonation feature as well as a magnetic influence detonator. In theory this device would cause the torpedo to explode as soon as it entered the magnetic field of a large mass of steel like a warship. If the detonation occurred underneath the keel of the vessel then the resulting upward explosion would break the back of the ship and send her to the bottom.

Unfortunately for American naval ordnance specialists, due to the differing nature of the Earth's magnetic field in relation to the ship's location on the surface of the planet, the magnetic feature of the exploder did not always work. The MK. VI performed well during testing at Newport News in Virginia's high 'magnetic latitude', but not so well near the earth's 'magnetic equator'.[i] The resulting number of dud torpedoes caused Admiral Nimitz to order the disabling of the magnetic feature on June 24, 1943. However, when the device's contact detonator was used in lieu of its magnetic feature, a secondary problem was discovered which was primarily a structural one. When the torpedo hit the target dead on, the housings that held the firing pin were crushed and did not allow the firing pin to strike and explode the charge. The solution to this problem was simply to replace the steel guide pins, which held the main firing pin, with aluminum ones; the lighter metal of the guide pins would now shear on contact, allowing the torpedo to explode.

The final difficulty presented by the Mk. XIV was not with the exploder but rather with the torpedo itself. When fired with a 'war shot' (the full-weight, explosive-filled warhead, rather than the lighter weight, calibration heads) the weapon had a tendency to run approximately ten feet too deep. The best solution for this error was to reset the depth features on all Mk. XIV torpedoes so that they ran at a depth that would allow them to hit the target rather than passing harmlessly underneath it.

On May 4, 1943, during USS *Wahoo's* fifth war patrol, an incident occurred that highlighted most of the troubles with American torpedoes. It was recorded as follows by Lieutenant Commander Dudley 'Mush' Morton in his war patrol report:

> Identified target as auxiliary seaplane tender … fired a divergent
> spread of three torpedoes … range 1,350 yards. The first torpedo

with Torpex head hit between the stack and the bridge. After a sixty-second run the second torpedo evidently passed ahead [of the target] and the third one fired aft must have been erratic. It is inconceivable that any normal dispersion could allow this last torpedo to miss a 510 foot target at this range.

The fact that most of these difficulties were discovered in the field by the boats' crews and then rectified at advanced bases by the serving line officers and men is a great tribute not only to the technical know-how of these men, but also to the general belief in the submarine service in the importance of team work.

Indeed, the navy was finding that many of its younger officers and crewmen were excellent, both in their fighting spirit and their technical expertise. Younger skippers like Dudley 'Mush' Morton of USS *Wahoo* would begin to change the tactics of the US Navy and bring a much-needed element of aggressive spirit to their missions. Officers like Morton used the high surface speed of their submarines to locate enemy vessels and race ahead of their intended targets to conduct their attacks.

One further positive result from the first two years of the War was that reports on the handling characteristics of new submarines had become available to the fleet from 1941. In the new Gato class, and its close sister the Balao class, many of the teething problems with engines and other equipment suffered by earlier US designs had finally been solved. Coupled with aggressive tactics, good crew training, and a reliable torpedo design the 'Silent Service' was about to make a great deal of noise in its prosecution of the war with Japan.

The men of US Navy submarine crews were a breed apart within the service, a fact that was often remarked upon by other members of the navy. A quiet and close-knit community, the men of a submarine crew were often likened to a family.

CHRONOLOGY

September 1776 *Turtle*, a one-man submersible vessel built by David Bushnell, attempts to attack HMS *Eagle* in New York Harbor.

July 1801 *Nautilus*, a submarine designed by Robert Fulton, makes a demonstration dive that lasts one hour.

February 17, 1864 *Hunley*, a confederate submarine, becomes the first vessel to sink another from a submerged attack when she sinks the sloop USS *Housatonic*. The *Hunley* is also destroyed in the attack.

1869 US Naval Torpedo Station, Newport, Rhode Island established.

1894 Whitehead-type torpedoes come into US Navy service.

April 11, 1900 Inventor John P. Holland sells the US Navy its first submarine; this event marks the beginning of the US submarine force. Later in the month USS *Holland* is commissioned as SS-1.

1911 The Bliss-Leavitt Mk. VII torpedo comes into service; this torpedo was to service the US Navy in the older 'S' class vessels until 1945.

March 1912 Lieutenant Chester W. Nimitz is appointed commander of the Atlantic submarine flotilla.

February 1914 USS *Skipjack* SS-24, the first American diesel-powered submarine, is commissioned.

1916 Plans for the new and faster 'S' class submarines are begun.

June 1916 The US Navy establishes the Atlantic submarine force.

January 1917 The submarine school at New London, Connecticut is founded.

June 1917 The US Navy establishes the Pacific submarine force.

1920–29 US Navy conducts experiments on chemical propulsion for its torpedoes.

1923 Naval Torpedo Station (NTS) obtains a monopoly on the production and development of US Navy torpedoes.

December 1927 USS *Paulding* SS-109 sinks off the coast of Massachusetts with the loss of 42 of her crew. The great loss of life leads to the development of special rescue gear like the McCann diving bell and the Momsen emergency breathing device.

June 1929 Charles B. Momsen assigned to the Submarine Safety Unit where he begins development of an escape device known as the Momsen Lung.

July 1929 Allan R. McCann assigned to the Maintenance Division where he begins work on the submarine rescue chamber that will eventually bear his name.

1931 The Bliss-Leavitt Mk. XIV torpedo comes into service in the US Navy – eventually over 12,000 of these devices will be produced by various manufacturers during the war years 1941–45.

1934 Navol, a chemical mixture of hydrogen peroxide, water, and alcohol is used in US torpedoes; the result is increased speed and range.

May 1939 USS *Squalus* SS-192 sinks during a practice dive, 33 members of the crew trapped aboard. US Naval forces commanded by Commander Momsen use the McCann diving bell to affect a rescue of the *Squalus* crew.

December 7, 1941 Japanese fleet units attack the US fleet at Pearl Harbor causing heavy loss to the American battle fleet.

December 8, 1941 US submarines are ordered to conduct unrestricted submarine warfare against Japan.

December 10, 1941 While undergoing overhaul at Cavite Naval Yard USS *Sealion* SS–195 is bombed and sunk during a Japanese air raid, the first US submarine loss of World War Two.

December 1941 to August 1943 'The great torpedo scandal' - American crews experience troubles with the Mk. XIV torpedo that include depth-running errors as well as faults with both the Mk. VI magnetic exploder and the contact exploder.

January 1942 Torpex, a new and more powerful explosive, begins to replace TNT in American torpedoes.

January 27, 1942 USS *Gudgeon* alerted via ULTRA sinks Japanese submarine I-173 off the coast of Midway, the

Admiral Charles Lockwood, known as 'Uncle Charlie' to the men of the Pacific submarine force, was the man largely responsible for making the fundamental changes in tactics that made the US submarine fleet so successful during the later half of World War Two. (NARA)

first US submarine sinking of an enemy warship in World War Two.

December 26, 1942 Lieutenant Commander Dudley 'Mush' Morton assumes command of USS *Wahoo* SS-238 and begins a series of war patrols that will make him a legend among the members of the silent service for his aggressive tactics and help to solve the problems that plagued the American Mk. XIV torpedo.

April 1942 to February 1943 Vice Admiral Charles A. Lockwood commands Submarine Forces Southwest Pacific, operating out of bases in Australia.

February 1943 Vice Admiral Charles A. Lockwood becomes commander of all submarines operating in the Pacific (COMSUBPAC).

February 7, 1943 Lieutenant Commander Walter Gilmore receives the Congressional Medal of Honor for his actions while in command of USS *Growler* SS-215 during her fourth war patrol. In planning a surface attack of what has been identified as a merchant vessel USS *Growler* is in turn attacked by what is in reality a vessel that has been converted into a Japanese gunboat. Gilmore turns *Growler* bow on to the gunboat and the two vessels collide at 17 knots. The gunboat rakes the bridge of *Growler* with machine-gun fire wounding Gilmore. Knowing that he will never make it

down the hatch in time, Gilmore gives the order 'Take her down' and thus sacrifices his own life to save his boat and crew.

March 1943 The first US homing torpedo, the Mk. XXIV (FIDO), goes into production.

1943 First electric torpedoes begin to arrive in Pearl Harbor (copied from captured German model).

June 24, 1943 Commander-in-Chief Pacific Forces, Chester Nimitz, orders the deactivation of the magnetic detonation feature on the Mk. XIV torpedo.

October 11, 1943 USS *Wahoo* SS-238 is sunk.

November 19, 1943 Captain Cromwell receives the Congressional Medal of Honor for his bravery while in command of a wolf pack; rather than risk important intelligence of the up-coming American attack on Tarawa falling into enemy hands, and knowing that through his capture the Japanese may be alerted to the US Navy's successful code-breaking efforts (MAGIC), Cromwell elects to go down with his command, the badly damaged USS *Sculpin.*

May 26, 1944 Commander Samuel David Dealey, Captain of USS *Harder*, receives the Congressional Medal of Honor for his exploits during *Harder*'s fifth war patrol when he sinks five enemy destroyers in five attacks.

July 30-31, 1944 Lieutenant Commander Lawson 'Red' Ramage receives the Congressional Medal of Honor while in command of USS *Parche* SS-384 as he sinks 14,000 tons of Japanese merchant shipping in the space of 46 minutes during a wild surface action against armed Japanese merchantmen.

August 23, 1944 USS *Harder*, while on her sixth war patrol, is lost to Japanese depth-charge attack along with all her crew, including Samuel Dealey.

October 22-23, 1944 While in command of USS *Tang* SS-306 on her fifth war patrol Richard Hetherington O'Kane receives the Congressional Medal of Honor for his aggressive surface attack on a heavily defended Japanese convoy.

October 24, 1944 USS *Tang* SS-306 is sunk by her own torpedo and O'Kane becomes a POW. This loss of an American submarine marks the first time that the Momsen Lung is used successfully as an emergency device to save the lives of US servicemen.

January and February 1945 Lieutenant Commander Eugene 'Lucky' Fluckey receives the Congressional Medal of Honor for his actions while in command of USS *Barb* SS-220 on her eleventh war patrol, when he aggressively attacks a Japanese convoy that has sheltered in a shallow harbor behind a minefield.

April 1945 Lieutenant Commander George L. Street III, while in command of the USS *Tirante* SS-420, receives the Congressional Medal of Honor for his audacious attack of a 10,000 ton Japanese tanker sheltering in shallow water, defended by two Japanese frigates which he also sinks.

August 6, 1945 USS *Bullhead* SS-332 is bombed and sunk, becoming the last US submarine lost in World War Two.

September 2, 1945 VJ Day ends hostilities in World War Two. US submarines have sunk approximately five million tons of Japanese shipping; 52 American submarines and 3,500 men are lost in the effort.

RECRUITMENT AND TRAINING

Perhaps it was the very character of America in the 1930s that attracted young men to the life of a sailor. The country, like most of the world, lay in the grip of the Great Depression and for many the future was exceedingly bleak. The US Navy seemed to offer an answer to that problem. For the recruit of a practical turn of mind the navy offered employment that would teach him a trade as well as provide him with shelter and a home. For those who sought release from the humdrum life of small-town America, the navy was an opportunity for travel and adventure. Indeed the phrase on the recruiting poster, 'Join the Navy and see the World', was a powerful inducement to these opportunity starved young men.

The greatest difficulty for a prospective recruit lay in being accepted into the service. The years before the War had seen massive unemployment and as a result there were far more applicants than vacancies. One potential recruit from the South recalled his despair when told by the navy recruiter of his district that the waiting list for recruitment had 300 names on it.

All successful naval recruits were volunteers between the ages of 17 and 25, unmarried, of 'good character', with letters of recommendation from their home town officials and able to pass physical, medical, and educational screening examinations. Naturally the competition was fierce and recruiters could afford to take only the best candidates. As a result the sailors that were taken into the submarine service were the 'best of the best'. One new recruit, James H. Hintzman, recounts his story:

> I enlisted in the USNR in Pittsburg, Pennsylvania and had to cram weight, eating bananas and [drinking] lots of water to meet their weight requirements.

US Navy recruiting poster that shows the combined glamour and mystery of the submarine service which made it so popular among recruits. (National Archives)

When war broke out with Japan in 1941 there was an immediate rush to join the navy in order to strike back at the nation that had bombed Pearl Harbor. Indeed, there were so many volunteers that the US Navy did not have to institute conscription until the end of 1942. Theodore H. Breisch, a student in college under a war deferment, wanted to get into the navy so badly that he deliberately flunked out of school in order to get into boot camp at Sampson Naval Training Station. Recruits gave many reasons for joining. Kenneth M. Jones, later a crew member of USS *Redfin* SS-272, volunteered to keep from being drafted into the Army. While Victor M. Radziwiecki, who later changed his name to Radwick, put it this way:

> I enlisted in March of 1942 because I thought it was my duty as a citizen of the United States to serve my country in its time of need.

When sailors were accepted into the service they were placed on the navy pay scale. For enlisted men the rates of pay varied from apprentice seamen who made $50 a month to chief petty officers at the top of the scale on $138 a month. Before the War, sailors serving on submarines received an extra $5 a month if they were non-qualified personnel, and an extra $20 when they became submarine qualified. Later, when the true danger of wartime submarine service was recognized, crew members received an additional sum of 50 percent of their base pay for 'hazardous duty'. Certain rates like sonar operators received an extra $5 a month on top of their base pay as an inducement to stay in the service.

Once inducted the recruit was issued his first set of uniforms, black silk neck scarf, a drawstring bag for his personal effects called a 'ditty bag', his sea bag where all these effects were to be stowed in lieu of a locker and, last but not least, the infamous navy hammock. Seaman recruit Joe Linick recalled his first experience with this contraption at Great Lake Naval Training Depot:

> We were issued white canvas navy hammocks and led into a large barracks with metal poles to which we tied our hammocks. Many of the guys had never slept in one before and we were often woken by the sound of one of them falling out of the hammock onto the deck.

Initially recruits were sent to basic training or 'boot camp'. Theoretically, this period of training lasted 16 weeks but due to the high wartime demand for crews it was reduced to six weeks of indoctrination, barely enough time to give the new recruit the minimal training needed to function as a part of the fleet. While in basic training the Navy instilled military discipline into the recruits and taught the individual how to think and act as part of a team.

The seaman recruits' daily routine began at 0530 with reveille and a series of brisk calisthenics. The day was divided into periods of drill, classes in navy protocol and physical training. Meals were served three times a day and the food was always plentiful if unimaginative; many 'boots', as the recruits called themselves, still have less than fond memories of the navy's creamed chipped beef on toast, known unflatteringly as SOS.

During their time in basic training 'boots' were given various tests to determine their aptitudes, with the better-educated or quicker recruits being sent to trade schools. These schools taught important skills from radar and radio operation to torpedo and fire control. The less skilful recruits would be sent directly to the fleet as unrated apprentice seamen and would learn their role in the navy the hard way.

Once with the fleet or at their trade school the new sailors were no longer 'boots' but they were still young men and most of them were away from home for the first time. Without supervision they could and did get into trouble. Richard Fason, an electrician who had been assigned as an instructor at the Class 'A' (which referred to the fact that this was the basic school for initial instruction) Electrical School in Sampson, NY describes his experiences:

> We had about 60 students bunked in our barracks; some of them not quite dry behind the ears and missed their mommies. There were a few rules in the barracks and one of them was lights out at 9.00pm; the first night there was pillow fight and noise long after lights out. The next night I woke them up at midnight, got them dressed, told them to grab their sea bag, and form up outside. There were no lockers in these barracks so everything was stored in their sea bags. I marched the men around the parade grounds two times with their sea bags on their shoulders. The next night ten minutes after lights out you could hear a pin drop on the barrack's floor.

Navy trade schooling lasted 16 weeks and was taught by senior chief petty officers, or CPOs, and other skilled petty officers who had been given their rating due to prewar expertise in their field. The lessons at trade schools were vigorous with the curriculum being equally divided between class work and hands-on experience.

Richard Fason, one of the school instructors, explains the classrooms and curriculum:

> The classrooms were well equipped with teaching aids and instruction books; we also had a large lab room with all kinds of electrical equipment. The lab was used one day a week for hands on training. I taught basic math, electrical theory and also, in the lab, how to operate and trouble shoot the equipment.

The top students in trade schools were given promotion as a reward for their performance, so the competition among the sailors to excel in their trade was very keen. Torpedoman Ron 'Warshot' Smith described the promotion system:

> Some of you [the top three] will get third class [petty officer third class, a rank equal to buck sergeant in the Army]. Ten more will get Seaman First and all of you will be promoted from Apprentice Seaman to Seaman Second, if you pass the class.[ii]

After graduation from the trade school the selection process for advanced training continued with volunteers being taken to submarine

school. Richard Fason finally received his transfer from 'A' school instructor to submarine trainee in this manner:

Early on in their training recruits were given classification tests to determine if they would be sent directly to the fleet or assigned for further skilled training. (National Archives)

> When I joined the navy I expected to be assigned to sea duty on a ship and see some action. After a couple of months as an instructor I got bored and turned in a request for transfer to submarine school to my CO. After about three weeks, I hadn't heard anything, so I went to his office to ask about it. He said, 'Fason, every week I take your request from the bottom of the stack, dust it off, read it, and put it back at the bottom of my in box … One day I saw on his bulletin board a notice wanting EMS [enlisted men] for submarine school … three weeks later I received my orders to report to New London Submarine School. My CO wasn't very happy that I went over his head but there was nothing he could do about it.

For others like Victor Radwick the choice of submarine school was less deliberate:

> Along with a group of other torpedomen, I was on temporary duty at the torpedo testing pier on Narragansett Bay, Rhode Island. I was assigned to the recovery gang. Our job was to hoist the just fired torpedoes from the recovery boat on to the docks. The job itself was not too bad but I was wet and cold all day long.

When the Chief in charge of our group informed us one day that our new orders had arrived … we actually had a choice of duty, become part of a new firing pier or volunteer for submarine school. I figured that water dripping off torpedoes at Montauk Point would be just as cold and wet so I volunteered for submarine school.

The selection process for this elite and dangerous training was rigorous; out of 100 candidates approximately one in ten would pass and be accepted into submarine school. Prior to final submarine school selection volunteers were subjected to a week of testing where they were evaluated for fitness. Due to the dangerous missions and difficult working conditions inherent in the submarine service, the tests were both physically and mentally challenging. Elimination from the program could occur for a variety of reasons, as veteran John W. Close Torpedoman 3rd Class relates:

Tests at submarine school were intense and given to the students on a weekly basis where a passing score needed to be 70 percent or better. (National Archives)

I volunteered three times and was rejected twice because of a lack of overbite in my teeth [deemed necessary to hold the mouth piece of the Momsen Lung firmly]. The third time the doctor tried to pull a rag from my mouth; he failed, and then passed me for submarine service.

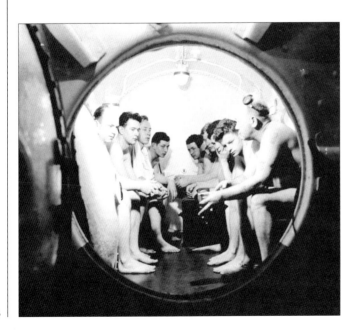

Night vision was also tested during selection. The potential submariners were brought into a darkened room designed to simulate the deck of a submarine at sea on a starlit night – as the sailors' eyes adjusted to the darkness, they would be asked if they could identify any shapes. If they could not see the vague gray ship silhouettes painted on the wall they would be dismissed from the school without prejudice to their career in the navy.

One of the more difficult and demanding tests was that of the pressure chamber. Here the seamen were subjected

One mandatory training activity prior to being taken into submarine school was the pressure chamber where men were given a test to simulate a submarine dive to 100 feet. (National Archives)

to conditions simulating those aboard a submarine submerged at a depth of 100 feet. The trainees were placed under 50 pounds of air pressure and 100 degree temperatures. They were monitored closely for signs of claustrophobia and stress; any sign of either would result in dismissal from submarine training.

For the final test the recruits were brought to the submarine escape tower, or 'the water works' as it was known to the men at the submarine school in New London, to perform a series of simulated submarine escapes. The tower itself was over 100 feet high and almost completely full of water. The trainees, clad in swimming trunks, were brought to the top of the tower, gathered around and given final instructions in the use of the emergency rescue device, known as the Momsen Lung. This device, named after its inventor Lieutenant Commander Charles B. Momsen, resembled a life vest filled with oxygen and was connected to a mouthpiece by a hose. The escapee would wear a set of nose clips and place the mouthpiece in his mouth. As he began to rise through the water he would breathe through the mouthpiece into the rubber bladder fastened around his chest. The air thus expelled would be chemically cleansed and allow the user an extra breath or two as they began the ascent.

The trainees were placed into a diving bell and lowered into the water through which they would make mandatory ascents from depths of 18 and 50 feet. Stationed in air-filled alcoves along the sides of the tank were experienced US Navy divers whose job it was to ensure the safety of trainees. After successfully completing the mandatory ascents, the trainees were offered the opportunity to try an escape from 100 feet. Whilst this was not a mandatory requirement for successful completion of selection, most of the budding submariners did make the attempt.

The trainees were brought back down the tower and led into a chamber at ground level. Set behind watertight doors, this chamber was designed to look like the control room of a submarine. From here the instructor turned a valve and began to flood the room until the water level reached the height of the trainee's armpits and the air pressure in the room had reached a level higher than that of the water pressure above the escape tube. No further water could leak into the room. The instructor then released a rescue

Instruction in emergency escape procedures was conducted in 100 foot escape towers located at US Navy submarine schools. Here a crewman is fitted with his Momsen Lung prior to an escape that will be made from the diving bell pictured in the photograph. (National Archives)

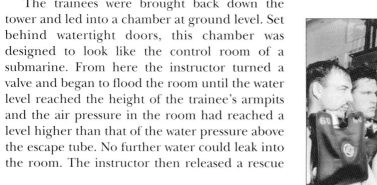

Following the loss of several submarines before the War the US Navy developed a special emphasis on rescue equipment. Here trainees are instructed in the proper wearing of the Momsen Lung. (National Archives)

buoy that shot to the top of the tower trailing an escape rope. The trainees would charge their Momsen Lungs and begin the ascent one at a time. Stationed along the sides of the tower the Navy divers watched over the trainees and looked for signs of disorientation or distress among them. John Close, a submarine sailor who did his escape training during the War at Pearl Harbor describes the experience in the tower:

> One by one the men, with their inflated Momsen Lung, ducked under the apron, climbed the ladder into the tank. The line released to the surface was held between your enmeshed fingers and thumb. You breathed into the lung and ascended, SLOWLY. There was a yellow buoy stop at 50 feet. You paused, took a breath into the bag; then ascended to another buoy at the 25 foot level; another breath into the bag; and ascend to the surface ... Accidents could happen if you panicked. However, the instructors were expert in spotting a potential problem, and could come to the rescue. At age 19, this was a lark, as well as good training.

At last, exhilarated by the experience, the trainees popped one by one to the top of the tank, swam to the side and hauled themselves out. They were one step closer to being submariners.

Prior to the war the navy had an extensive submarine training program at the submarine school in New London, Connecticut. Here trainees and veteran sailors who wanted to join the submarine service were introduced to 'Spritz's Navy', the nickname given to the school in honor of the infamous CPO Charles Spritz, a senior enlisted man at the facility. Spritz, a martinet, was a former New York City policeman and charged with the discipline of the newly indoctrinated submarine trainees. He set about his task with fervor. It is fairly safe to say that, because of his hectoring by-the-book ways, CPO Spritz was one of the most hated men in the navy. He allowed no margin for mistakes, no matter how trivial the circumstance. New men were taught the rigors of the submarine service with this choice motto:

> Around here there's only one daily prayer. You'll commit it to memory: Oh, Lord help us keep our big mouths shut until we know what we are talking about.[iii]

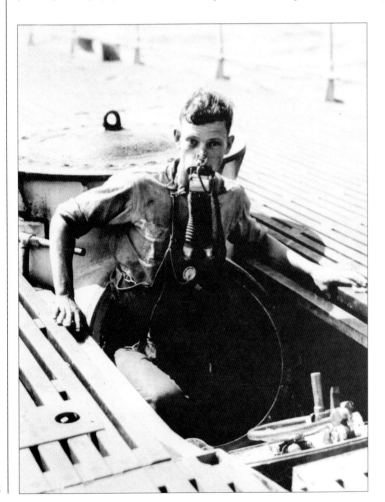

A crewman demonstrates the proper method of wearing the Momsen Lung as he moves from the aft escape trunk in this prewar photograph.
(US Navy Photograph)

Under Spritz's regime even experienced men were treated like they were back in boot camp and they resented it. Yet in order to succeed at the school they had to endure the harsh, punctilious actions of the Chief without complaints, otherwise they would not pass and would be returned to the fleet. Despite Charlie Spritz and his kind, most if not all of the trainees found the experience of the submarine school to be a positive one. Richard Fason described the experience in this way:

> In Spritz's Navy you either shaped up or shipped out. I heard the scuttlebutt and tried extra hard to pass. Spritz kept everyone's liberty card in his office. To get off base, you lined up outside Spritz's office for inspection. He checked your shoes, uniform, and haircut; if all was in order, you got your card. You had to be in good shape of body and mind, but I made the grade.

A typical day was based around four hours practical work and four hours of classroom lectures. The students were divided into 'dive sections' of six to eight students under the direction of a single CPO, who remained with the group for their entire stay at the school.

The daily classes that the trainees attended were tough, taught by experienced Chiefs, and covered all the systems that a sailor would encounter on a submarine. While in New London the trainees were required to maintain workbooks containing sketches of all the systems that they had learned about. Monday was given over to tests on the previous week's lessons and the sailor had to pass with at least 70 percent; failure of two exams led to removal from the school. Richard Fason described an incident in his learning experience:

> The base had a theater where training films were shown to all the students at the same time. One day we were watching a film on buoyancy … when it was almost finished the commander walked in and found most of us sleeping or nodding off. He ordered that a test be given to all of us immediately after the movie was over. If you failed it you were restricted to base. There wasn't much sleeping in the theater after that!

During the war it soon became apparent that the number of trained submarine crews was insufficient to compensate for losses and the navy's own policy of mandatory crew rotation following war patrols. The submarine school at New London sought to alleviate this

One of the first skills to be taught to seaman recruits at boot camp was the basic proficiencies of knot tying; here 'Boots' learn the art from a Chief Petty Officer, or CPO in navy terms. (US Navy)

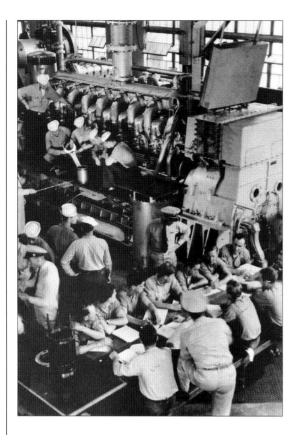

The training curriculum for US submarine crews was quite extensive with both textbook as well as 'hands-on' experience as demonstrated in this image of the diesel repair laboratory in New London, Connecticut. (National Archives)

problem by increasing the speed of the training with the use of advanced combat simulators. The three areas of the submarine that the simulators focused on were the conning tower with the attack teacher, the control room's diving trainer, and the torpedo room. All of these devices were mock-ups of the equipment to be found in a submarine and included mechanical features that would simulate the motions of the boat in diving and combat conditions. Consequently, even before stepping aboard, the trainees would have an idea of how to operate the boat's important controls and systems.

In the fourth week of training the fledgling submariners were at last given their first ride aboard a submarine. The school boats were old, obsolete vessels of the 'O' and 'R' class, designed and built during or immediately following World War One. The first dive was normally short, no more than ten minutes, but it was a white-knuckle experience for most of the trainees. As claxons sounded, orders for the dive were given, the crew moving with silent efficiency to demonstrate to the new submariners the realities of running the ship. Torpedoman Ron 'Warshot' Smith put it this way:

A voice over the loud speaker called out 'dive, dive.' The throbbing from the diesel stopped … a mess attendant came into the mess hall as the boat began to tilt sharply down at the bow … he smiled and walked over. 'Nothin' to be afraid of. Ain't no big deal, but it's OK to be a little scared cause sometime the dives don't go exactly like they's 'posed to.'[iv]

Antiquated submarine designs, like this 'O' class were utilized as training vessels at navy training schools. (National Archives)

Gradually, as the dives grew longer the trainees were instructed in the proper operation of the boat's systems. The training teams that crewed the boat rotated assignments and after about a dozen dives, each section would have experienced all aspects of running the boat. Theoretically, all of the trainees had to be able to operate all the systems of the boat in case of emergency.

Graduation day from Spritz's Navy was one of great exaltation for the students, not only because they were released from the iron regime of the school but also because upon graduation they would be given two weeks' leave prior to their new submarine assignments.

SUBMARINE ASSIGNMENT AND CREW LIFE

Graduation from the submarine school at New London did not automatically mean that the new submarine sailors would be assigned to a boat. Following their two-week leave members of the graduation class might be assigned a variety of tasks – some would continue on at the school as crew for the training vessels; others would be sent to the advanced 'C' schools in their area of specialty. EM 3/C Fason was sent to Gyrocompass school in Brooklyn, New York:

> After leave I was sent to school for four weeks. The instructor was very good at teaching and I enjoyed the class so I studied extra hard. I asked the instructor so many questions that I think he was happy to see me go when BuPers [Bureau of Personnel] assigned me to the USS *Queenfish* SS-393 then under new construction.

A significant portion of the new graduates of submarine school were immediately sent overseas to join relief crews either serving off of submarine tenders or working at the repair facilities.

The job of the replacement crew was straightforward. When a boat returned from war patrol, the relief crew took over from the regular ship's company to make any necessary repairs or refurbishments. Bernard Schwartz, who was to become famous under the pseudonym Tony Curtis, was a member of a relief crew serving aboard USS *Proteus* AS-19. He recounted that:

> Whenever a sub came in after a war patrol, they would tie-up along side, and go on liberty. Our job as relief crew was to go aboard and clean it up, scrape the barnacles from the sides and assist in whatever repair work was needed.[v]

The final group of graduates was sent to 'new construction', meaning that they would journey to one of the country's shipyards and become part of the crew for a new submarine that was being built.

New construction was one of the plum jobs of the submarine service and as a consequence was highly sought after by officers and crews alike. It meant that the crew would be involved with the 'fitting out' of a new boat. Barracks space was provided at the yard, often aboard a special 'barracks' barge moored alongside the dock. Officers and crew would arrive in batches and be assigned to 21 days of 'New construction school' by the executive officer or XO, whose main responsibility was the material readiness of the boat. The XO also supervised the further training of the crew as they arrived at the navy yard, some of whom would be sent for

When submarines returned from war patrol the regular crews departed their boats for rests; while they were gone repairs to submarines were conducted by replacement crews, usually new men, prior to their assignment to a ship's company, with a few veteran hands mixed in to make sure the work was done correctly. (National Archives)

further schooling. When the boat was finished the crew would be allowed aboard to learn the systems of the new boat.

Once the vessel was launched the original crew members, known by navy tradition as 'plank owners', would spend their days running through a variety of exercises designed to simulate most of the situations a crew would experience while at sea. This occurred while the boat was tied up at the dock. Rigging for sea, rigging to dive, action surface, fire and collision drills would be practiced over and over until they became second nature to the crew.

Once the boat was in working order she would be taken for a series of practice dives to see if all systems were fully functioning and that there were no material faults in the construction. At Mare Island it was common for boat captains to insist that the construction crew came along with the crew on the initial hull-testing dives to ensure that the civilian contractors had done the best-quality job possible. It was at this point, following the practice dives, that if the boat had passed all tests and was deemed to be in good material condition it was formally accepted into navy service by the captain.

Boats that were built at the East Coast facilities normally conducted their training cruises in safety areas within the confines of the Gulf of Mexico as they made their way down to the Canal Zone prior to

USS *Balao* SS-285, one of a new class of vessels that entered service in 1943 and were constructed of high-tensile steel which improved the depth to which the vessel could safely operate, down to 400 feet. (US Navy Photograph)

deployment to the Pacific theater, where the major US submarine effort was being made. During this last peaceful time the crew settled into the routine of daily life aboard a wartime submarine.

The typical crew of a 'fleet' boat in the mid-war period consisted of six officers and 50 crew members, numbers being increased as circumstances dictated, perhaps to serve additional new electronic gear, for example the SJ Radar. Thus, by 1945, the size of the typical submarine crew had risen to eight officers and 62 enlisted men.

THE OFFICERS

At the top of the hierarchy of the submarine chain of command was the captain, commonly called the 'Skipper' or even, regardless of age, the 'old man'. The title 'Captain', when applied to the skipper of a submarine, was a courtesy afforded to a man whose actual rank was more likely to be Commander or even Lieutenant Commander. This officer was ultimately responsible for the boat and the decisions made during war patrols - he would use the periscope, plan and execute any attacks and was responsible for how well the boat executed its missions with the fleet. Torpedoman Billy Grieves of USS *Thresher* SS-200 described one of his captains:

> Our skipper CMDR William L. Anderson was relieved and transferred back to the States and our new skipper CMDR William J. Millican reported aboard. Captain Millican was a short man on the stocky side, and very aggressive. He had been a championship boxer in the Naval Academy. As the crew got to know him, every man would willingly follow him anywhere.

At the start of the War many commanding officers of submarines were full Commanders who had taken the long, slow route to promotion in the peacetime navy. Most of these men were over 35 years of age and had been imbued with the safe and cautious tactics that were prewar navy doctrine. As a result when war broke out and they were authorized to wage unrestricted submarine warfare against Japan many of them were not equal to the task. To successfully fight this kind of war a different type of officer was needed – someone who was more aggressive. Starting early in 1942, therefore, the older officers were replaced by younger men in their late 20s to early 30s. Normally Lieutenant Commanders, these younger officers brought much-needed aggression and dash to the submarine service. Six of these new submarine skippers would receive the Congressional Medal of Honor: Samuel Dealey, USS *Harder*; Eugene Fluckey, USS *Barb* SS-220; Gilmore, USS *Growler* SS-215; Richard O'Kane, USS *Tang* SS-306; Lawson Ramage, USS *Parche* SS-384 and George Street III, USS *Tirante* SS-420.[vi]

In a speech given after the War at a tribute lunch to honor wartime submarine skippers, Billy Grieves of USS *Thresher* summed up the most important quality that a skipper had:

> What was this rare innate quality our skippers called upon to handle such formidable responsibility? Was it guts? Could you call

it that? Evel Knievel [a motorcycle stunt rider] has guts and guts can be foolhardy. Guts can be fatal. It took more than guts, it took unshakeable determination. It took superb competence. It took unprecedented concentration. On life or death missions there are no rules; success rests on leadership and composure.

Next in the chain of command was the executive officer, or XO; if the skipper of the ship is the father of the family then the XO is the mother, responsible for the day-to-day routine of the vessel. He oversaw the various departments of the submarine together with the classes that were held to qualify all crew members. These classes, called the 'school of the submarine', were designed to take the new man through the entire boat and teach him every system aboard. In theory to be qualified in submarines a man had to have working knowledge of every part of the boat. Formal classes were usually conducted by submarine-qualified officers, and the men were required to keep workbooks that documented their progress towards qualification and contained diagrams and notes of the systems on board that they had studied. Finally, after much hard work, a crewman was given a comprehensive written test and a practical exam where he was expected to solve problems and demonstrate knowledge of the boat and its systems. Most XOs also functioned additionally as navigation officer, tasked with the problems of getting the boat from one port of call to the next, and the maintenance of accurate navigational logs.

It was important that relations between skipper and XO were good. If all went well then the combination of the two made for a happy, well-handled boat; if, however, there were difficulties between the two then the efficiency and safety of the submarine could be in jeopardy. The saga of USS *Wahoo*'s first two war patrols provides evidence of the necessity for a smoothly functioning team.

Commanders needed to be careful approaching targets even at periscope depth as the tell-tale wake would alert sharp-eyed enemy lookouts to the submarine's presence. (National Archives)

Wahoo set out from Pearl Harbor on her first war patrol on August 23, 1942 with Lieutenant Commander Marvin G. Kennedy in command and Lieutenant Richard O'Kane as XO. Assigned a patrol area around Truk Island, Kennedy almost at once began to demonstrate two traits that were fatal in a submarine skipper – over-caution and poor boat handling – so that the confidence of officers was shaken. On two separate occasions *Wahoo*, with Kennedy at the con, missed opportunities to fire at major Imperial Japanese Navy (IJN) warships passing through the patrol area, as *Wahoo*'s first war patrol report explains:

September 30 - 0520: Sighted ship later identified as Aircraft Tender *Chiyoda* … range 12,000 yards. Estimated target was headed for the Piaanu Pass and that we were in ideal attack position … We turned to normal approach course and closed the range to 6000 yards at which point we were on 130 degrees starboard tack. Weather was ideal for a submarine attack and we were able to watch the target continuously except when making high speeds to close range. There were no screens or escorts … the Japs were just begging someone to knock off this Tender, but it was not our lucky day.

Kennedy's reliance on the submerged approach had allowed the Japanese ship to slip away unmolested. A similar incident occurred again on October 5, 1942:

Sighted aircraft carrier *Ryujo* [misidentified, as this vessel had already been sunk by carrier planes]. Accompanied by two Amagiri class destroyers … range 11,000 yards, speed 14 knots. One DD was leading and the second was trailing carrier. Made approach which, upon final analysis, lacked aggressiveness and skill, and closed range to about 7000 yards. Watched the best target we could ever hope to find go over the hill untouched.

Indeed the first war patrol report by Kennedy chronicles a series of miscalculations (including the accidental firing of an armed torpedo while the vent doors were still closed) that brought his handling of *Wahoo* into question. Returning to Pearl Harbor on October 17, *Wahoo* was made ready and set sail on her second war patrol on November 8. Accompanying *Wahoo* this time, however, was Lieutenant Commander Dudley 'Mush' Morton in the role of Prospective Commanding Officer or PCO. Normally, the PCO would watch and learn, but as the second patrol developed into a repeat of the first it became apparent to the XO, O'Kane, that Morton was the better choice as commander, combining aggressiveness with a certain 'killer instinct' that was wholly lacking in Commander Kennedy.

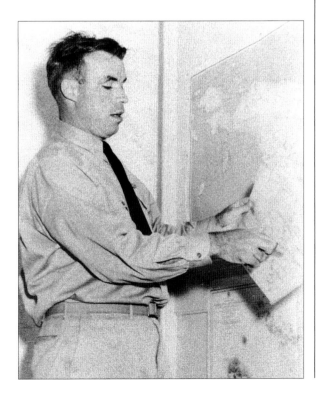

Lieutenant Commander Dudley 'Mush' Morton was one of a new breed of submarine officers who broke away from the cautious prewar submarine attack doctrines of the US Navy; he began a series of aggressive war patrols aboard USS *Wahoo* that ultimately inspired such officers as Richard O'Kane, recipient of the Congressional Medal of Honor. Morton was killed in action on October 11, 1943. (US Navy Photograph)

23

When *Wahoo* was ordered to Brisbane, Australia at the end of her second patrol, all three of the officers in question were interviewed by Rear Admiral Charles 'Uncle Charlie' Lockwood, the commander of submarine forces in the southwest Pacific. O'Kane and Morton's evaluations of the patrol were highly critical of Kennedy – when asked by Lockwood what he would do Morton reportedly replied: 'Shoot the yellow SOB.' Whether or not this was actually said it was certainly in character with Morton's no-nonsense attitude and Kennedy was relieved of command. Morton duly became the new commander of USS *Wahoo*.

The four other officers in the chain of command of a submarine were the engineering officer, the diving officer, the communications and commissary officer, and the gunnery and torpedo officer. Each of these men were the heads of their respective departments and responsible to the executive officer for the training of the crew under them and the smooth-running daily routine of their department.

The engineering officer, normally a senior Lieutenant, was responsible for the function and maintenance of the boat's propulsion systems. These included the four main diesel engines, used while the boat was on the surface, and the electric motors used for undersea propulsion. The main engines were four ten-cylinder diesels that could produce 1,600 horsepower and push the submarine along at a maximum speed of 20 knots while on the surface. The battery powered electrical motors were rated at slightly over 1,300 horsepower and could propel the submarine at speeds of up to nine knots when the boat was submerged.

The next in the chain of command was the diving officer, who might either be a Lieutenant or a Lieutenant Junior Grade (JG), and was tasked with maintenance of the boat's underwater handling characteristics. Once a day the boat would make what was called a trim dive, where the taking on or pumping out of water in what were called the trim tanks adjusted the balance of the boat. The aim of this dive was to give the boat neutral buoyancy so when she was submerged she would maintain a set depth, without additional controls or propulsion being applied.

The communication and commissary officer was either a Lieutenant JG or an Ensign. Communication was a heavy responsibility on a submarine because, once under way, coded transmissions were constantly received. The submarine would normally maintain radio silence once on patrol, so communication was limited to the decoding of the messages sent to them from the fleet. Because of the Allied success in breaking Japanese codes (MAGIC), many of these messages would include exact locations and compositions of Japanese convoys.

The torpedo and gunnery officer was another junior officer's billet, whose job was to supervise the torpedomen and the training of the gunners for the boat's secondary armaments and anti-aircraft guns. Along with his weapons responsibilities, the junior officer aboard the boat was also '1st Lieutenant', a non-command designation that meant that in addition to his regular duties he was also responsible for the outer appearance of the vessel while she was in port.

'The torpedo room is manned and ready.' While the torpedo was the main weapon of the submarine, the torpedo room also served as berthing space for part of the crew, 13 in the forward room and 11 in the aft torpedo room. On long war patrols the crew of the aft room would hope that the captain would fire as many stern shots as possible to relieve the cramped conditions and allow the crew to make more bunk space. (US Navy Photograph)

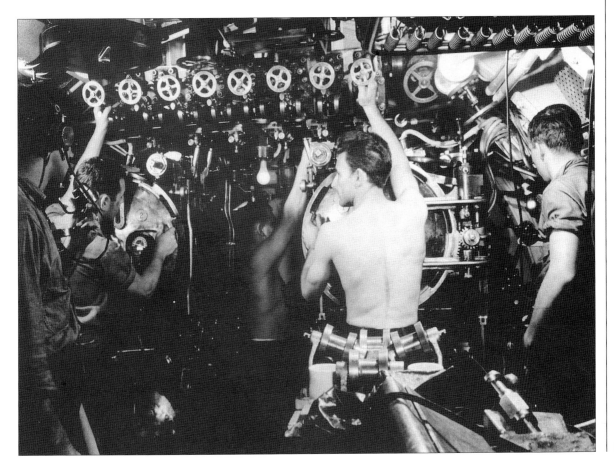

Victor 'Rad' Radwick, a torpedoman aboard USS *Guavina* SS-362, described relations between officers and men this way:

> The relationship between officers and men was as informal as it possibly could be, very light and casual. One reason for that possibly was that officers did not have a 'watch-day' attitude. They gave an order, and then promptly forgot about it, for they knew it would be carried out. There was no need to 'double-check' the men. Consequently trust between officers and a man was automatic, not forced. The relationship between the Captain and the crew was a bit more formal of course, but still nothing like it was aboard the larger ships or at a base.

THE MEN

The bulk of the ship's company was made up of 50 to 60 enlisted rates and six to eight Chief Petty Officers or CPOs. Similar in composition to the hierarchy of officers the CPOs were headed up by the senior chief, who had the title of chief of the boat, or COB. The chief was the senior enlisted man and acted as the crew's representative reporting directly to the captain. Generally speaking the COB was an older man with years of experience behind him, able to harass men if they were not up to scratch, but still approachable. The COB generally had more authority than the junior officers because he was a veteran, qualified in

Officers and crew alike often grew beards during lengthy Pacific patrols. Here the officer on the deck of USS *Batfish* SS-310 keeps a close lookout. (US Navy Photograph)

Life aboard a US submarine was crowded and in general something was always going on in all parts of the boat. Here a quartermaster sews a set of battle flags representing the number of vessels the submarine has sunk, while a torpedoman performs routine maintenance and a crew mate takes an opportunity to get some rest in his bunk. (US Navy Photograph)

submarines, and they, most probably, were not. Torpedoman Ron 'Warshot' Smith USS *Seal* SS-183 describes his COB this way:

> Chief Hickman was a nice guy, typical of most COBs. They had the knack of getting along with everyone and were usually well liked.[vii]

The rest of the complement of six to seven CPOs might be and usually were from a gamut of the trade specialties. USS *Guavina* SS-362 at one point had a torpedoman, a boatswain, an electrician, and a motor machinist amongst her chiefs.

Before the War, CPOs were predominantly professional seamen of vast experience. According to Ron 'Warshot' Smith:

> They were Asiatic sailors, not unlike the French Foreign Legion. Professional military men, many had joined the navy to stay out of reform school. Others had joined up to get away from an angry father, because they had knocked-up his daughter. It had been so long since most of them had set foot in the United States they did not feel it was home anymore. The navy was their home.[viii]

By late 1942, however, most if not all of these career 'old salts' had been transferred to duty in the training schools, allowing them to pass their knowledge and experience on to the younger generation. Replacing them was a group of younger men only a few years older than the majority of the boat's company – World War Two would be a young man's war.

An ammo passer removes a 5-inch shell from the forward service locker during a surface action drill. US submarine crews were a casual lot with regard to dress while at sea, as shown by the non-regulation wearing of the crewman's 'Dixie cup' hat. (US Navy Photograph)

For the most part members of the enlisted ranks were young men ranging in age from 17 to 25; many of them had enlisted immediately after the Japanese attack on Pearl Harbor. The attitudes of the crew toward the enemy, however, varied. To many of them the Japanese were an enemy to destroy in any way possible, while others felt far more sanguine about their job. This is how a few sailors on fleet boats explained matters – Victor Radwick:

> I don't think that I really gave much thought of how I felt about the Japanese. Along with the rest of the officers and crew, I wanted *Guavina* to sink Japanese ships and to survive their attacks upon us. I suppose that our survival was always in the back of our mind whether we realized it or not. For the most part however, was the simple realization that we had a job to do and the sooner the job was done, we could go home.

Electrician's Mate 2nd Class James H. Hintzman, USS *Redfin* SS-272, echoes Radwick with this sentiment, "I don't recall having any personal animosity toward the people we were fighting until we heard stories of their barbaric treatment of our prisoners."

In a more direct vein Motor Machinist Mate Kenneth M. Jones was quite clear on his feelings about the enemy, "We was happy after every ship that we sunk, of course we hated the Japanese."

The crews of wartime submarines were remarkably close knit, with the confines of the boat serving to reinforce these bonds. While on war patrol the majority of the crew would not set foot out on deck for 30 to 40 days – their existence would be the 'routine' of the boat. As they neared the area of their patrol zone, the days and nights of the crew would be reversed. The boat would dive shortly before dawn and the crew would spend the day underwater, engaged in their evening activities. Surfacing after it was dark, the engine room would be a scene of hurried activity as the main diesels would fire up and begin the task of charging the batteries. During the long daytime routine boredom would quickly set in if the crew were not in action. Victor Radwick explains:

> A typical day's routine aboard a sub while on patrol was just that … routine. After days and then weeks at sea, it often became quite boring. As part of the deck crew my duties varied depending on whether we were submerged or surfaced. While on the surface my primary job was that of lookout but I also spent some time at the helm. While submerged I alternated between the helm and the bow and stern planes, and one of the sonar devices.

The relationship between the crewmembers was very close. Working together in such confining quarters necessitated complete

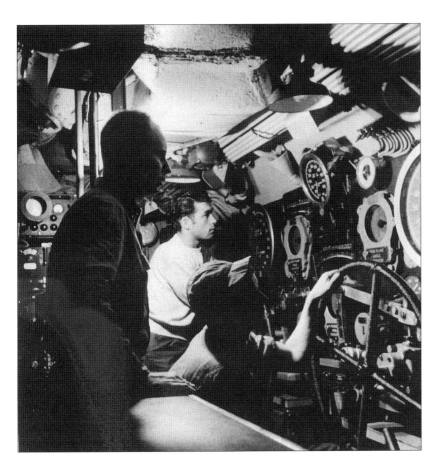

cooperation with one another. We had to put aside petty grudges, personality conflicts, differences of opinion, anything that would create a problem of getting along. We had no choice to do otherwise for each man was depending on someone else to do his job as well as he did his own.

The watches for the crew were divided into sections of four hours on and eight hours off. Members of the crew not qualified in submarines would catch up on their work to learn the boat's systems, while others caught up on their sleep or relaxed with the old navy standby of a cup of 'Joe' and a game of cribbage. While gambling was strictly against the rules the routine often left little else to do, and many crew members won fabulous fortunes from their less lucky mates … all to be paid back 'after the war'.

Another vice that was strictly forbidden by navy regulations was the consumption of alcohol, but 'where there's a will, there's a way'. Whether it was called 'jungle juice', 'hooch' or 'torpedo juice', there was always a supply of illicit liquor

aboard a submarine, the key ingredient of which was the alcohol that was used in the fuel for the torpedoes. The brew was never good but taken in small amounts it helped the crew to pass the time and break some of the monotony.

One skipper, Medal of Honor recipient Lieutenant Commander Eugene 'Lucky' Fluckey in his fine book *Thunder Down Below* tells of how he kept one of the showers of the USS *Barb* stocked with cases of beer, to be broken out as a reward if and when they sank an enemy ship. No doubt that can of beer made for a fine incentive as well as a great morale builder amongst the crew of the *Barb*.

Richard Fason from USS *Queenfish* SS-393 explained his experience with 'torpedo juice':

> I was responsible for the gyrocompass and cleaned the carbon that formed on the rings every two weeks with pure grain alcohol. The captain kept a gallon locked in his stateroom for that purpose. Paul Miller the COB would get a half a cup from him when it was time to clean the compass. I used a spoonful [to clean the compass] and we put coke syrup in what was left over and drank it!

Food was another great morale builder aboard submarines and due to the difficult nature of submarine duty the navy always tried to ensure that the food or 'chow' was the best. Three regular meals were scheduled during the day and they usually coincided with the changes of the watches. Those going on watch would be served first, then those off watch, and finally members of the crew who were coming off watch. According to most submarine veterans, sandwiches and snacks were available at most times and of course the ubiquitous navy coffee. The only problem with the food aboard a submarine was in the quantity they

This photograph shows the intensity of the surface watch while on patrol. The officer in the foreground wears the US Navy foul-weather, waterproof pullover made from rubberized canvas. (National Archives)

were able to carry. Normally the crew would start out a patrol eating steak, fresh vegetables and baked food, but after 40 days they would be down to powdered eggs and canned potatoes. Victor Radwick, USS *Guavina*, describes the food situation this way:

> Storage facilities on a submarine were very limited and this lack of space was a problem because it severely curtailed the amount of fresh foods, such as meat, vegetables, milk, and eggs.
>
> Despite these limitations the meals aboard a sub were well prepared and plentiful. Submarine cooks and bakers were very gifted and resourceful and cheerfully gave us what we wanted.
>
> Toward the later part of our patrols we became more and more dependent on canned goods, which were placed behind every pipe, valve, gauge, wherever it would fit, throughout the boat. Thus the quality of our meals at the end of the patrol tapered off.

Surprisingly, even though the air on the boat had very limited circulation, cigarette smoking was allowed even while the boat was submerged. Everyone on board would breathe easier when the boat surfaced at night and, with the opening of the hatches, sweet air from topside flooded into the boat in a great rush. An apocryphal story is told by submarine crews about two sailors attempting to smuggle a baby skunk aboard the boat as a new ship's mascot – when questioned by the captain about the smell they replied, 'Don't worry, sir, he'll get used to it.' Needless to say, the air aboard a submarine was often a foul combination of mildew, sweat, diesel oil and cigarette smoke.

This 1943 photograph shows a nice assemblage of insignia common to submarine crews. Four of the five of the enlisted men have been awarded the Silver Star for their accomplishments, and visible on all of the uniforms is the submarine qualification badge – white dolphins embroidered on uniform cloth – worn on the lower right cuffs of the uniforms, as well as the submarine combat badge above the ribbon bar. The two sailors on the left wear their rating patches on their right sleeve which indicate that these two men are deck sailors, while the other two enlisted ratings have their rank on the left sleeve indicating that both are below-deck sailors, with the sailor (second from the left) being a Machinist's Mate 2nd Class.

LIBERTY AND LEAVE

The types of authorized absence from the boat fell into the two broad categories of Liberty and Leave. The official navy definition of Liberty is: permission to be absent from the ship or station for a period of up to 48 hours, or 72 hours if in case of a three-day weekend. Anything of longer duration is termed leave. Before the War it was common practice, while in port, to allow most of the off-duty crew liberty provided they obeyed the rules of the port. This practice changed during wartime, however, when the massive influx of soldiers, sailors, and marines to a port could swamp the available local resources, and it became necessary to send sections (about a quarter) of a crew on liberty at any one time.

When arriving fresh from the States the crew of a new boat would not be entitled to the longer two-week rest and recuperation leave that was customarily granted to boats just back from war patrols. Because of this the crew of new boats were only granted liberty while the boat finalized preparations for getting under way on her first war patrol.

Liberty ports themselves varied in the degree of comfort and amenities that they provided. Places like Honolulu, Brisbane, and Perth were popular because they were large cities and virtually any form of entertainment could be catered for. Because some of these ports were close to the war zone they had strict curfews – Honolulu, for example, had a curfew at 1800. Liberty there normally commenced at 0900 and the crews lucky enough to have a pass were allowed off base. While on liberty the sailors were allowed to go pretty much anywhere on the island. Because of its beaches and warm water, Waikiki was popular for swimming and surfing. The Royal Hawaiian Hotel right on Waikiki was the rest camp for submarine crews just back from war patrol and it provided lavish food for the men.

The first stop for many sailors would be a tailor's shop where they would purchase new uniforms. Skin tight everywhere except the bell bottoms of the pants, these new blues or whites sported the submarine qualification patch on the arm and fancy embroidery on the inside of the cuffs which, contrary to regulations, the sailors tended to wear turned back. With new smaller Dixie cup caps worn well back on their heads, sailors would stop and have their pictures taken with their buddies and maybe even a hula girl with a Hawaiian paradise backdrop. Younger sailors might get tattoos from one of the many parlors that dotted the landscape.

Most of the off-duty personnel sooner or later made their way to the downtown establishments in and around

A submarine crewman enjoys a beer and a burger at Camp Dealey following a war patrol. In the warm weather of the Pacific theater submarine crewmen were allowed two beers a day while resting at a forward base – needless to say this was a rule that was often ignored by the crews. (National Archives)

In Quarters

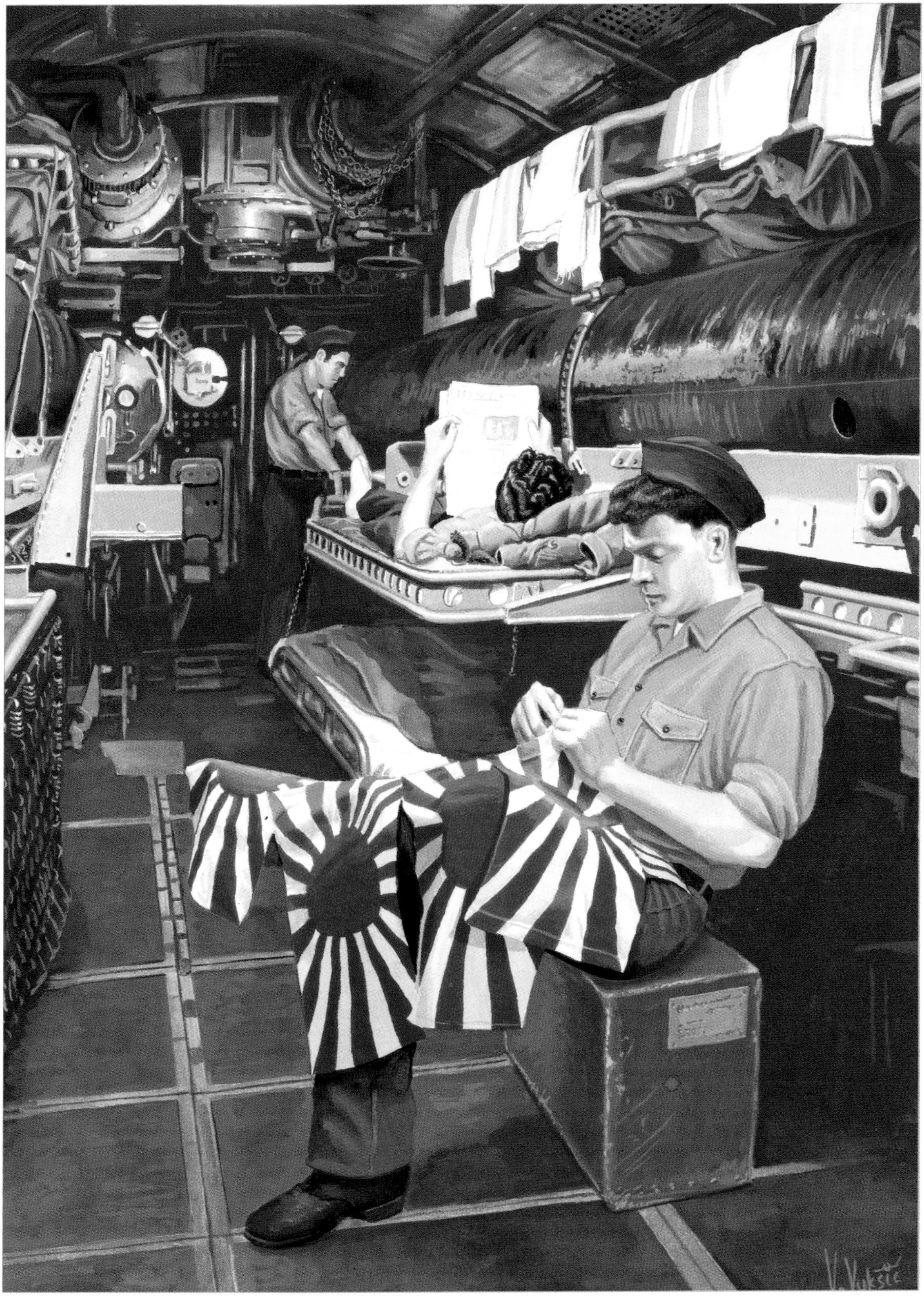

A

B

Loading Torpedoes

c

Torpedo Launch Diagram

D

E

F

Night Action

G

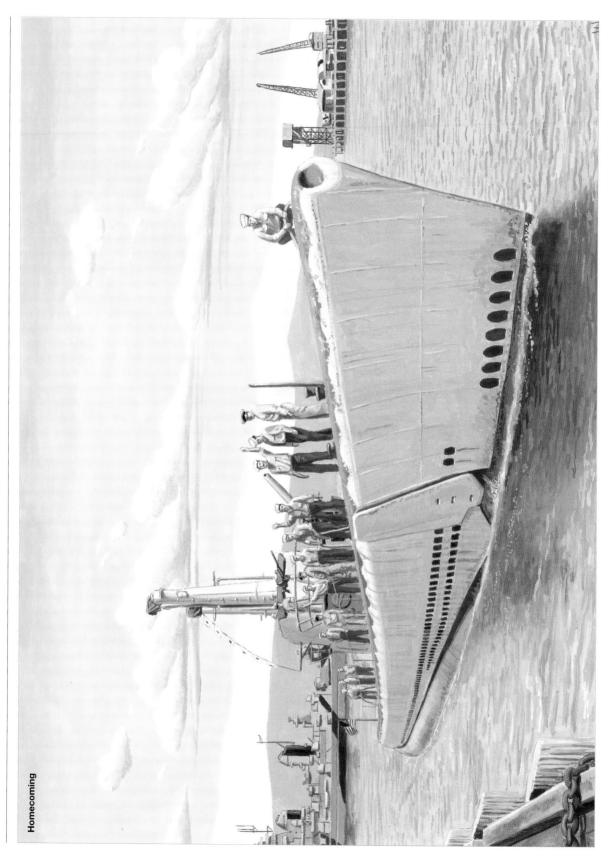

Hotel Street. This area was known for its rough characters and was notorious for its many brothels, bars, and gambling dens. Here, among places with such picturesque names as WO Fat's and the Black Cat, sailors would undergo a test of endurance, both moral and physical. Curfew as previously mentioned was at 1800 with a general lights-out blackout being imposed. Most of the bars in the Hotel Street district wanted to have a quick turnover in clients so many of them imposed a two-drink limit on visiting sailors before they had to 'shove off'.

Prostitution was legal in Hawaii and carefully regulated by both the military and the Honolulu police. An official price was set at three dollars a head. At one point during the War prostitutes went on strike for an increase in prices, but the Provost Marshal of Hawaii maintained that to charge more was unpatriotic considering the low pay of the average enlisted man, and broke the strike. If a sailor was inclined for such a promiscuous adventure then he would have to join one of many long lines in front of the door leading to the 'bull ring', a local term for the brothels.

Returning crews had rooms at the Royal Hawaiian Hotel where the men would sleep four to a room. The rules at the Royal Hawaiian were very strict and navy personnel were not allowed to have any females in their rooms; likewise the curfew of 1800 was enforced by Marines detailed to guard the hotel grounds.

Other liberty ports were equally esteemed by submarine crews, Perth in Western Australia being a particular favorite because of its small size and the fact that their were far fewer military personnel around. Victor Radwick recalls one liberty 'down under':

> One particular liberty that stands out in my mind was at Perth in Western Australia. Because of a typhoon in the China Sea our departure from our station off Camrah Bay, French Indo-China was delayed long enough that we did not make port by Christmas, arriving on 27 December.
>
> However, we were looking forward to a big time on New Year's Eve. Unfortunately it fell on a Sunday and everything in Perth was closed, the pubs, restaurants, and even the movies. So Joe Arway, George Ketchersid, and I gathered up all the snacks such as potato chips, pretzels, cold cuts, crackers, beer and wine we could lay our hands on, enough to fill three large boxes. We then proceeded with boxes on our shoulders strolling along the streets of Perth looking for female companionship. It was tough, for the streets were almost deserted of all foot traffic. Finally we stumbled on three women from the Australian army … anyway they agreed to spend New Year's Eve with us. We spread a blanket over the grass at a park and celebrated!

Not all liberty and rest stations were as desirable as Honolulu, Brisbane and Perth; some like Midway could be downright barren. Situated as it is between the main naval facility at Pearl Harbor and the Japanese home islands, Midway was the logical place to build an advanced base for submarines and establish a rest station for crews awaiting repairs to their boats. Unfortunately, for the crews of the boats and the tenders working out of Midway there was very little on the

Crew members from USS *Batfish* SS-310 take time to get some sun while in port. One of the minor problems for submarine crews was the inability for most of them to get on deck and catch a breath of fresh air while on patrol. (National Archives)

island from which to build the right facilities. Midway and its neighbor island, aptly named Sand Island, were just that, mainly sand. Everything needed to build a base had to be brought directly to the island from the United States.

The rest facilities at Midway consisted of one primary structure: the old Pan American Hotel. In previous years this building had served a variety of people as they stopped over on the long Pacific flights in the Pan Am 'China Clipper' flying boat, including the Japanese ambassador returning home following the attack on Pearl Harbor. But those days of travel were long gone and the hotel, now christened the 'Gooney Bird Hilton', was home to returning submarine crews. The hotel gained its nickname from the island's only other commodity, the albatross, or 'Gooney' bird that raised its young in thousands on Midway's sandy beaches. Officers and men alike were given billets at the 'Gooney', enlisted men in the one wing and officers in the other. The enlisted men shared billets, usually four to a room, whereas the officers might, if they were lucky or of high rank, have a room to themselves. Junior officers would more likely bunk up with another officer. But whatever its disadvantages, the 'Gooney' did provide the men with real beds and daily showers. Later in the War, as the base grew and the number of submarines operating out of Midway rose, an entirely separate building was built to house just the officers of these returning boats.

Recreation on Midway was makeshift and consisted of swimming, shell collecting on the beaches and impromptu sports activities like baseball games between crews. The men had plenty of money to spend from their accumulated pay and every night there was gambling in the lobby of the hotel. As previously mentioned, navy regulations forbade gambling but at the 'Gooney Bird Hilton' a blind eye was turned to this activity and even officers got involved. Card games like blackjack and poker were the most popular and were played with table stakes, meaning that you brought a certain amount to the table and when that was gone you were out of the game. Really large sums of money could be won by men whose futures were in doubt and who tended to be reckless. Unfortunately for the winners, navy regulations would only allow a sailor to send a $50.00 postal order home at any one time, so if you won you either had to carry the cash around with you or find some trusted buddy heading back to the States to carry it with him and deliver it.

Ship's services ran a store on the island where the men could buy candy, gum, and cigarettes at 50 cents a pack. Likewise, the ship's services store provided one case of beer a week to the men of each particular room in the 'Gooney'. The beer was warm and bore such unappetizing names as 'Blats' and 'Green River', but it was better than nothing and the crews soon found ways to cool the cans in the waters of the Pacific.

With so many young men all grouped together with little to do other than drink, trouble was bound to start. Ron 'Warshot' Smith in his book *Torpedoman* recounts the following tale of a baseball game that got out of hand:

The next day they organized a baseball game, the Seal men against the crew of the Runner. The game started O.K. The chiefs of the boats acted as umpires and everyone was having a

Following the Battle of Midway the island was turned into a forward supply and repair base for submarines moving from Pearl Harbor to Japanese waters. Submarine crews ashore rested at the former Pan Am Hotel, nicknamed by the men the 'Gooney Bird Hilton'. (National Archives)

good time. As the beer started to take effect, the arguments got louder and shoving matches started ... By the seventh inning no one was sober enough to know what the score was, or care and a real fight broke out. The men in the bleachers from each side jumped in. Almost a hundred men were hitting and wrestling each other.[ix]

A great many tensions were released by crews on liberty and rest leave and no doubt people were hurt on account of it, but these men were about to go back to one of the most dangerous theaters of operation: the undersea struggle against Japan.

WAR PATROL: THE UNDERSEA WAR AGAINST JAPAN

In order to understand a typical war patrol aboard a US submarine operating in the Pacific, it is necessary to consider, on a year-by-year basis, the strategic setting in which these warriors operated.

1939–41: Plans and Preparations

The United States was not at war with the Axis nations at this time, however, as the War began to go badly for the Allies it seemed clear that Roosevelt's pledge to keep America out of the War was going to be difficult to keep – if not impossible. With the fall of France in June 1940, Franklin D. Roosevelt saw clearly that America must increase its cooperation with Great Britain and prepare for war.

German submarine activity in the Atlantic was both a threat and an opportunity for the US Navy – a threat because of the risk of losing American shipping to German submarines and the corresponding loss of US lives that might drag America into the War; while an opportunity

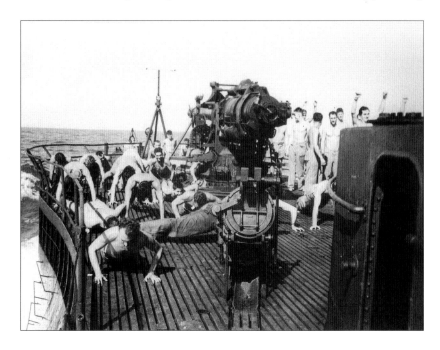

Some of the larger prewar US submarines like USS *Nautilus* and USS *Argonaut* were used to carry out special missions such as carrying US Marines from Carlson's raiders back from a special raid on Makin Island in August 1942.

was presented when US Navy units began joint convoy escort duties with the British to protect neutral shipping. In so doing the navy could hone its anti-submarine skills and share valuable information with its British counterparts.

In the Pacific, American commanders, certain that war with Japan was on the horizon, began to formulate their own contingency plan. War Plan Orange had as its central tenet the fact that Japan would attack the Philippines first. The plan envisioned the garrison of the Philippines fighting a holding action and slowly withdrawing down the Bataan Peninsula as they awaited reinforcements from the American fleet at Pearl Harbor; the role of American submarines was to scout for the fleet and destroy any IJN surface forces that they encountered.

1941–42: Holding the Line

The Japanese attack on Pearl Harbor changed the nature of American war plans in the Pacific. Although War Plan Orange was sunk along with the American battleships, the Japanese had by no means achieved all their objectives, for the attack failed to destroy three major targets: the American carriers, the fleet's fuel reserve and the American submarine bases at Pearl Harbor.

For American submarine forces the change in plans was immediate as they set out to 'wage unrestricted submarine warfare on Japanese merchant targets'. More realistically, American submarines and aircraft carriers were deployed to defend the line that ran from Pearl Harbor to Midway, and the Aleutians in the north. They probed Japanese defenses, scouted for the main fleet and picked off the occasional Japanese warship. The first year of the War was, however, a disappointing time for American submarine crews.

By the late spring/early summer of 1942 Japan was prepared to renew its offensive in the Pacific. Choosing New Guinea and Midway Island as their targets the Japanese fleet was poised to strike.

Acting on information gained from operation MAGIC (the code-breaking program directed against Japan), Admiral Nimitz gathered his weaker forces and parried both Japanese attacks with a combination of skill and surprise. Both New Guinea and Midway were saved and the tide of battle in the Pacific turned in favor of the Allies. With the Japanese reverse at the Battle of the Coral Sea and the defeat at Midway, Allied forces began their first advances against the Japanese, at Guadalcanal in the Solomons.

1943–1944: Island Hopping

Immediately following the American victory at Guadalcanal two plans of advance were under consideration and there was much contention for the adoption of one plan over the other. The first plan, for an advance in the southwestern Pacific, was advocated by General Douglas MacArthur and had as its goal the liberation of the Philippines. The second plan was conceived by Admiral Chester Nimitz, and was to hop from one Pacific island to the next as American amphibious forces breached each successive line of Japanese defenses. In reality, decisions for the adoption of one plan or the other were never made, for America, with its immense material superiority over Japan, chose to follow elements of both plans.

During this period American submarines were employed in two roles. In the first role, prior to amphibious landings, they conducted reconnaissance missions ahead of American forces. In the second role, in order to weaken the garrisons of the islands that the Americans planned to attack, US submarines sank Japanese merchant ships carrying supplies and reinforcements.

It was during this crucial phase of the War that American submarines were at last freed of the torpedo glitches that had so hampered their earlier efforts. The number of Japanese merchant ships sunk increased and, as the raw materials that these vessels carried never reached Japanese factories, the dual effort of America's strategic bombing and the undersea blockade began to bring Japanese industry to a halt.

1945: The Final Act

As soon as America and her allies had established forward air and sea bases during the island campaign they began the strategic and systematic destruction of Japanese industry. American B-29s flying from newly won bases on Saipan could reach any part of the Japanese homeland.

By late 1944 American submarine forces engaged in the strangulation of Japanese merchant trade had been largely successful and in the final phase of the War American submarines took the conflict directly into Japanese home waters, enforcing a tight blockade on Japan. In the last year of the War the Japanese were forced to take extreme measures to supply their factories – they employed small native fishing boats to carry war materials in an attempt to sneak these smaller, less tempting targets past the waiting American submarines. US submarines increasingly operated on the surface as 'gunboats', stopping and searching these vessels and sinking them with gunfire if necessary.

Figures for 1945 show the grim success achieved by the unrestricted submarine warfare campaign against Japan: in total nearly five million tons of Japanese merchant shipping was lost during the War. Following the dropping of the atomic bombs, which made the invasion of Japan unnecessary, American submarines were present at Tokyo Bay for Japan's formal surrender.

BOATS ON PATROL

As boats received their orders and prepared for a war patrol, new crew members realized that their months of hard training were about to pay off. For the first few days after receiving orders, officers and men loaded the stores and munitions that they would need on their long patrol. Perishable foods were brought on at the last possible moment in order to keep them fresh. In order to maximize the storage of provisions, canned goods were stashed in every nook and cranny, the diving officer noting the weight of each item so that he could swiftly adjust the boat's trim when they were under way. The complement of 24 torpedoes was taken aboard and stowed in the forward and aft torpedo rooms.

Both the captain and the executive officer would go through crew rosters and see if the boat was at full compliment, adding any new arrivals if necessary. The 'Doc', normally a Pharmacist Mate, would

check everyone's health and recommend any replacements that might be needed. Almost everyone had heard the stories of 'Doc' having had to take out an appendix at sea, but nobody wanted to have first-hand experience of the procedure.[x] Then with everything loaded and everyone aboard the boat would cast off and make its way out of the harbor towards open sea.

In order to safeguard the boat from American air patrols, standard operating procedures stipulated that the boat should be escorted from the harbor and a little way out to sea by an American surface vessel. It was well known by boat crews that 'zoomies', as the pilots were called, often dropped their bombs first and waited for verification of a target's identity afterwards; so the presence of the destroyer was a welcome comfort. Later, when they had reached a predetermined point, the boat would make a trim dive to check the neutral buoyancy, and the surface ship would drop a practice depth charge close to the boat to accustom the crew to the sound of an explosion – hopefully, the only time they would hear one. From this point on the submarine was alone and every contact would be treated as hostile.

Lifeguard duty following heavy air raids was an arduous task for submarine crews, but the rewards could be remarkable. USS *Tang* SS-306 under the command of Lieutenant Commander Richard O'Kane rescued 22 fliers following the Truk raid of April 1944. (US Navy Photograph)

Submarine tenders provided all maintenance and supply for submarine divisions while on war patrol from advanced bases. USS *Holland* AS-3 is shown in this photograph with boats from Submarine Division 15.

After the initial departure from Pearl Harbor, course would be set for Midway Island. Midway was now the American advanced submarine base in the Pacific where the crew would top off fuel, add a bit more fresh food and receive orders for their patrol area. Past Midway, boats would begin the reversed schedule of diving during the day and surfacing at night in order to make a speed run and charge their batteries. Often no specific orders were given to the boat once it reached a patrol area, so the captain could react as opportunity allowed.

Although the Americans had broken the Japanese naval code early in the War, decoded information had to be used with care. Boats could only be directed to Japanese targets when a sinking would not endanger the secret of the American code-breakers. Captain Cromwell even chose to go down with USS *Sculpin* when she was fatally damaged rather than risk the possibility of being taken prisoner and being forced to divulge the secret of operation MAGIC.

For the first two years of the War US submarines operated alone and did not adopt the wolf pack tactics of German U-boats. Many of the more successful skippers like Richard O'Kane and 'Mush' Morton were uncomfortable with the restrictions that the pack commander was likely to place upon them. Yet by 1943 the wolf pack was becoming a regular feature in American tactics.

The procedure was for the pack, which normally consisted of three boats, to make their way separately to the patrol area. Once on station the pack commander, a captain with the temporary rank of Commodore, would direct his submarines to their assigned patrol stations, which were fairly wide apart to avoid accidental attacks on friendly targets. Here the individual captains would take over and conduct their attacks either on the surface or underwater as they saw fit. All the boats would maintain strict radio silence except to share information on contacts that were too far away to be attacked but heading towards a pack mate.

Attack Procedures

The first contact between submarine and target was likely to be made with the new surface search SJ radar. SJ radar was installed on most American submarines by late 1942 and allowed the submarine to make intermittent readings on contacts up to 20 miles away, and more reliable readings on contacts in the 8 to 10 mile range. The early sets were notoriously finicky and were difficult to read and calibrate, yet they

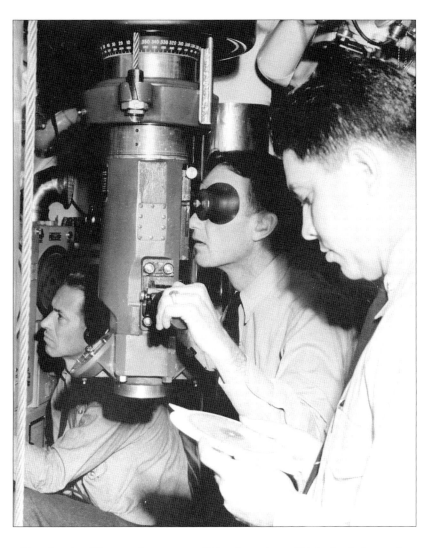

offered a significant advantage to US submarines. With the information provided by the SJ radar the skipper would have a range of options for the attack approach. If weather conditions were favorable the boat would stay on the surface and use its 20 knot speed to make an 'end run' around the target, maneuver itself ahead of it, submerge and wait until the target crossed its path before firing.

The submarine would now adopt its normal approach course, positioning the target vessel on the submarine's beam at a right angle to the target's bearing. The skipper would make periodic checks of the target's range and speed using his periscope-mounted ST radar. He would then estimate the angle on the bow of the target and the line-of-sight range which were fed in to the Torpedo Data Computer or TDC, automatically generating a firing solution for the torpedoes. Once the initial estimates of target distance, speed, and angle on the bow had been fed manually into the TDC the machine would automatically track the target and make adjustments to the torpedo gyros. Optimum range was figured at 1,000 yards with a zero-degree gyro angle on the torpedoes and a track angle (the angle between the torpedo's course and the target's course, usually 70 to 120

In this 1945 photograph torpedo crews load a Mk. XIV torpedo into the forward torpedo-loading hatch of a fleet-type submarine. American submarines carried 24 such torpedoes while on war patrol. (US Navy Photograph)

degrees) of about 100 degrees. Having achieved the best firing solution possible the skipper would order the torpedoes to be fired. Firing could be done singly or, to increase the chance of scoring a hit, in a spread of more than one torpedo.

Once the order to fire the torpedoes had been received crews would open the breech door of the tube and load the torpedo manually. The tube was then flooded with water from a tank on the boat and the outer or muzzle door opened. Compressed air would be forced into the tube expelling the torpedo on its run, the outer door was closed and the sea water in the tube allowed to drain into a holding tank.

Sonar would track the 'fish' to the target, and if all was well, the words 'the torpedoes are running hot, straight, and true' would be relayed to the captain. Normally, a manual track of the target was also kept by the torpedo officer with a hand-held device known as an 'is/was' along with a stopwatch to follow the exact running time. If all went well with the firing procedures then the torpedo would hit the target and the next sounds that the sonar man would report would be the 'breaking-up' of the collapsing bulkheads as the target sank.

Victor Radwick describes in vivid detail one such attack during USS *Guavina*'s SS-362 fifth war patrol off Camrah Bay in Indo-China:

We encountered a tanker of some 8,500 tons being escorted by three destroyers. The presence of the destroyers presented a formidable risk for us to attack and the fact that the convoy was hugging the coast and therefore in shallow waters made the attack even more of a challenge. This did not prevent our skipper, Ralph Lockwood from making the attack on the tanker ... our torpedoes found their mark and the tanker was sent to the bottom. Because we were only in 130 feet of water we could not

USS *Sea Dog* SS-401 engages in surface action drills with the 5-inch gun mount. The power of the 5-inch gun was excellent for engaging Japanese tankers carrying highly volatile crude oil, likely to explode when being hit. (US Navy Photograph)

dive deep, our best defense against depth charge attack. We had no choice but to settle on the bottom and prepare for the worst.

The three destroyers attacked with a vengeance dropping strings of depth charges all day long, a total of 98 … Aircraft also joined in the attack dropping several bombs at many intervals.

We were now what is called 'silent running' which means that all equipment is turned off, including the circulation of air and no one moves around unless absolutely necessary, the lack of air circulation caused breathing difficulty and the boat became very hot and uncomfortable … I have no doubt that to a man, despite our usually cocky attitude that 'our boat' could take anything that the Japanese could throw at us, now and then during the attack some element of fear crept into our hearts.

At last, as darkness began to settle outside, the Japanese broke off the attack and left the area … we surfaced and to quote an old expression 'got the hell out of there'.

The length of time spent on a war patrol varied, with the normal length being 40 to 60 days, although such determining factors as the expenditure of all the boat's torpedoes or a major material defect that prevented the safe operation of the boat might cause a boat to head for home. Whatever was the case, when a boat returned from patrol every effort was made by the submarine command to make the members of the returning boat's crew feel welcome.

One welcome sight for returning US submarine crews in the Pacific theater was the Golden Gate Bridge in San Francisco. Here a number of crew from USS *Batfish* SS-310 smile at the sight of it as the submarine heads for the San Francisco–Oakland Bay Bridge. Following extended wartime service in the Pacific submarines were routinely returned to the submarine repair facility at Mare Island near San Francisco. (US Navy Photograph)

Crews themselves were immensely proud of their boat's accomplishments while on war patrol and made 'unofficial' battle flags for their submarine that recorded the various successes that they had achieved while at sea. Small Japanese pennants, the rising sun for IJN vessels and the 'meatball' for merchant ships, denoting the tonnage sunk, would be strung along the anti-fouling lines that stretched from the fairwater on the conning tower to the bow of the boat. The proudest display that any submarine could make was a broomstick at the periscope shears, showing the whole submarine fleet that the boat had made a 'clean sweep' and sunk all enemy vessels that they had encountered.

When at last they had tied up to the pier, accompanied by the strains of navy band music, the boat and its crew were welcomed home by the brass – often Admiral Charles Lockwood himself, the COMSUBPAC, known affectionately to the men as Uncle Charlie. In the days that followed, the boat was turned over to the replacement crew who would see to any repairs while the crew took a well deserved two weeks of rest and recuperation leave at the special facilities that were prepared for them. During this time COMSUBPAC evaluated their mission and the skipper's war patrol reports. If all was in order then the mission was deemed a success and the officers and crew would be entitled to wear the submarine combat patrol badge.

Other Missions: Lifeguard, Raids and Recon, and Surface Actions

Submarines performed a variety of missions while on war patrol so it is a serious error to conclude that all their missions were anti-shipping operations. American submarines and their crews were very versatile in what they could accomplish. For further information on the above types of mission the reader is directed to the color plate write-up that covers each topic.

Aboard USS *Nautilus* these two Marines were part of the Makin Island raid. Of interest is the 6.5mm Japanese Arisaka infantry rifle one of them has 'liberated' as a war souvenir. (National Archives)

SELECT SUBMARINE AND NAVY GLOSSARY

Ash can depth charge.

Baptize to fail to flush the pressure toilet on a submarine properly; see also head and chocolate chipped.

Battery compartment there were two on each fleet boat; the after battery compartment was the main bunk space for the crew and the forward battery compartment was 'officers' country'. In both cases the electric batteries were stored under the decks in the two spaces.

Betty a Japanese Mitsubishi G4M2 bomber.

Bravo Zulu Navy flag message that denotes a job well done.

Broach to come to the surface out of control.

Can slang for a destroyer; also called a 'tin can'.

Chocolate chipped – the results of a failed effort to flush the head properly; see also head and baptize.

COB Chief of the Boat, the senior CPO.

COMSUBPAC Commander Submarines Pacific.

During the course of the War numerous Allied soldiers became prisoners of war in the hands of the Japanese where they were forced to work as slave labor. Here Allied POWs are rescued by an American submarine after it had torpedoed the Japanese transport that was taking them to Japan. (National Archives)

Con the control of the boat.

CPO Chief Petty Officer, the Navy equivalent of a sergeant in the Army.

Doc the Pharmacist Mate who took care of the medical needs of the crew.

Dolphins the badge worn by submarine-qualified crew, officially gold for officers and embroidered for crew; some of the men bought unofficial silver badges in Australia for wear with work uniforms.

Dud a piece of ordnance that had failed to explode.

Fish nickname for a torpedo.

Gee dunk ice cream, candy, potato chips, and the place where they can be purchased.

George the junior officer aboard a boat, given all the extra and unwanted tasks by his superiors.

Gooney Bird the nickname given to the albatross on Midway; also a slang term for the Douglas C-47, or DC3 aircraft.

Head the toilet on a submarine; see also baptized and chocolate chipped.

JG stands for Lieutenant Junior Grade, one rank above Ensign, just below full Lieutenant.

Mail buoy a fanciful term used to fool new recruits about staying in touch with the outside world while on patrol. According to scuttlebutt the Navy would keep track of the boat and drop a mail buoy with news from home.

MOMM Motor Machinist Mate also know as MOMAC.

OOD Officer of the Deck, responsible for the safety of the ship while on watch.

Periscope shears the structure atop the conning tower that supports the periscope, a favorite place to station topside lookouts.

Pig boat early submarines, no doubt a reference to the smell.

Run war patrol.

Scuttlebutt a rumor.

SD air-search radar.

Sewer pipe a slang term given to the inner pressure hull of the boat.

SJ surface-search radar.

Skipper the old man, the captain of the boat.

Smoking lamp the term used to tell a sailor whether he was allowed to smoke or not; the lamp is said to be lit if permission is granted.

SS abbreviation in navy registration and classification for submarines. Also the later version of air-search radar that replaced the SD equipment.

TBT Target Bearing Transmitter, a binocular-like device used for aiming torpedoes while on the surface.

TDC Torpedo Data Computer, the mechanical device that worked out the correct firing solutions for a torpedo once programmed. One TDC could operate all the tubes on board.

Torpex the explosive in American torpedoes that replaced TNT.

Trim the longitudinal balance of the submarine while under water.

Ward room the place where officers take their meals and socialize.

War patrol a run of about 60 days in a war zone.

Wolf pack a group of submarines operating together.

XO Executive Officer.

Zero bubble the term given to the level trim of the boat when submerged; thus to keep a zero bubble is to keep one's head and not get carried away.

Zig-zag to steer a non-straight course with one's vessel to avoid torpedoes.

Zoomie a pilot of an aircraft.

While not often used during the War due to the fact that submarines operated in blackout conditions, searchlights were standard equipment on all US submarines. (US Navy Photograph)

MUSEUMS AND COLLECTIONS

For those interested in the history of the US submarine service there are a number of museums around the United States. The list below contains just some of those museums and collections and makes no pretence at being complete.

The Boats

USS *Bowfin* SS-287
Pacific Fleet Submarine Memorial Association
11 Arizona Memorial Drive
Honolulu, HI. 968818
The display contains USS *Bowfin* SS-287, a World War Two fleet boat restored to wartime configuration. The park also boasts an indoor museum that contains displays of submarine artifacts, battle flags, and other memorabilia.

USS *Pampanito* SS-383
National Maritime Museum Association
PO Box 4703310
San Francisco, CA. 94147
Pampanito is the most complete fleet-type submarine open to the public. While aboard the visitor has a sense that she is ready go on war patrol. A very active veterans' group is associated with the boat and will often invite veterans aboard to speak about their recollections of the silent service.

USS *Cavalla* SS-244
Seawolf Park
Pelican Island
2102 Seawall Blvd.
Galveston, TX. 77550
Open to the public is USS *Cavalla*, a famous fleet boat that was credited with sinking the Japanese carrier *Shokaku*. *Cavalla* is in 1960s configuration and is a good example of the conversions that the fleet boats underwent to extend their service life.

USS *Clamagore* SS-343
Patriot's Point Naval and Maritime Museum
40 Patriots Point Road
Mount Pleasant, SC. 29464
Patriot's Point is the home of numerous vessels of interest to the student of World War Two, including the USS *Yorktown* CV-10, USS *Laffey* DD-724, and USS *Clamagore* SS-343. *Clamagore* herself was one of the last diesel-powered boats to see service in the US Navy.

USS *Drum* SS-228
USS Battleship *Alabama* Commission
PO Box 65 Mobile, AL. 26601
The Battleship Memorial Park's main display is of course the battleship *Alabama* BB-60, of the South Dakota class of vessel. USS *Drum* is a famous *Gato* class submarine moored at the park, open to tours by the public. The Memorial Park also boasts a fine collection of Second World War aircraft and vehicles.

USS *Silversides* SS-236
Great Lakes Memorial and Museum
PO Box 1692
Muskegon, MI. 49443
USS *Silversides* is a Gato class vessel that is credited with being the third highest scoring boat in terms of tonnage sunk during the War. The park also contains the Coast Guard cutter *McLane* and LST 393.

USS *Cod* SS-224
Cleveland Coordinating committee for the USS *Cod* Inc.
1089 East St.
Cleveland, OH. 44114
USS *Cod* is a Gato class boat that has been left in wartime configuration. Operating out of Australia during the War *Cod* is famous for her wartime rescue of the crew of the Dutch submarine 0-19.

USS *Ling* SS-297
State of New Jersey Naval Museum
PO Box 395
Hackensack, NJ. 07601
The museum features USS *Ling*, a Balao class boat together with Japanese and German midget submarines.

USS *Lionfish* SS-298
USS Massachusetts Memorial Battleship Cove
Fall River MA. 02721
Lionfish is a Balao class boat open to the public along with USS *Massachusetts* BB-59 and the USS *Joseph P. Kennedy* DD-850. The park also contains two restored PT boats from World War Two, PTs 617 and 796.

USS *Cobia* SS-245
Wisconsin Maritime Museum
75 Maritime Drive
Manitowoc, WI. 54220
USS *Cobia* is on display at Manitowoc, WI. The

Loading a Mk. XVIII torpedo onto a US submarine. Beside the torpedo is a 5-inch/.25-cal. Mk. XL deck gun. During the War the US Navy experimented with a variety of deck gun configurations to find the most suitable weapon. (US Navy Photograph)

home of the shipbuilding facility that built 28 submarines during the War. Along with *Cobia* the facility has a museum with silent service exhibits and a museum library.

The Submarine Force Museum
NavSub Base, New London
Groton, CN. 06349
This is the official Submarine Museum of the United States Navy and as such houses a large collection of both submarine artifacts and a library of submarine-related material and photographs. On display at the museum are the USS *Nautilus* SSN-571, the first nuclear submarine, and four World War Two midget submarines.

St Mary's Submarine Museum
102 St. Mary's Street West
St Mary's, GA. 313558
St Mary's museum is a facility that serves all eras of the silent service, from the creation of the first submarine to the modern ballistic missile submarine. Included among the displays are working periscopes and a submarine simulator.

Naval Undersea Museum
610 Dowell St.
Keyport, WA. 93845
The museum serves many purposes with displays about undersea exploration and technologies.

It has a very extensive collection of torpedoes that span the years from their invention to the modern day.

The Navy Museum
805 Kidder Breese Street
Washington Navy Yard
Washington DC, 20374
The Navy Museum is a facility that covers the entire history of the US Navy and has a section devoted to the silent service in World War Two.

Ben Bastura's Submarine Museum and Library
440 Washington St.
Middletown, CN, 06457
1-860-346-0388
A private collection of submarine models and memorabilia that ranges from books and historical files on US submarines to a collection of 300 patches, plaques, and photos of American submarines. The collection is open to the public by appointment.

SELECT BIBLIOGRAPHY

Blair, Clay, *Silent Victory: The US Submarine War against Japan*, J.B. Lippincott Co., Philadelphia and New York, 1975.

DeRose, James F., *Unrestricted Warfare: How a New Breed of Officers Led the Submarine Forces to Victory in World War II*, John Wiley & Sons, New York, 2000.

Holmes, Harry, *The Last Patrol*, Naval Institute Press, Annapolis, MD, 1994.

LaVo, Carl, *Back from the Deep: The Strange Story of the Sister Subs Squalus and Sculpin*, Naval Institute Press, Annapolis, MD, 1994.

Mendenhall, Corwin, *Submarine Diary: The Silent Stalking of Japan*, Naval Institute Press, Annapolis, MD, 1995.

Smith, Ron, *Torpedoman*, a private publication, 1993.

Stern, Robert, C., *US Subs in Action*, Squadron/Signal Publication, Carrollton, TX, 1979.

Sumerall, Robert, *Warship Data 6 USS Bowfin (SS-287)*, Pictorial Pictures Publishing Company, Missoula, MT, 1999.

NOTES

[i] Milford, Fredrick J., 'US Navy Torpedoes', *The Submarine Review*, April 1996.

[ii] Smith, Ron, *Torpedoman*, 1993, p. 11.

[iii] LaVo, Carl, *Back from the Deep*, 1994, p. 16.

[iv] Smith, *Torpedoman*, p. 28.

[v] 'Tender Tale of World War Two – and a Young Man Serves his Country', Oral History, Bernard Schwartz (http://www.missippi.net/~comcents/comcent/tendertale.com)

[vi] The asterisk indicates that the individual received the medal posthumously.

[vii] Smith, *Torpedoman*, p. 46.

[viii] Smith, *Torpedoman*, p. 54.

[ix] Smith, *Torpedoman*, p. 91.

[x] Pharmacist Mate Wheeler B. Lipes, USS *Seadragon* SS-194, actually did perform an emergency appendectomy on 19-year-old Darrel Rector during the boat's fourth war patrol.

PLATE COMMENTARIES

A: IN QUARTERS

When stationed aboard a submarine the sailor had to be aware that he would be in close confines with the rest of his shipmates. Special care had been taken in the selection of the crew for these long voyages and a certain amount of family-like feelings developed among the crew. Never while on shore leave or liberty would an observer see a member of a submarine's crew alone - they were a tight-knit and closed-mouth bunch.

Visible in this plate is a scene from a home-bound boat; the sailor in the foreground is busy sewing the tally flags that show the success of his boat on the current war patrol while his mates relax with a game of cribbage and a quiet moment with a magazine. Early in the patrol conditions in the torpedo room would not be quite so comfortable when the boat carried a full set of torpedoes and the crew were forced to hot-bunk, meaning that they shared sleeping space so the bunk never had time to get cold. Crew stationed in the fairly cramped quarters of the aft torpedo room would often beg the 'Old Man' to fire a few stern shots in order to place a few more bunks.

B: TRAINING

Submarine crews got the most pay out of all the branches of the navy; this was due in part to the extra amount of training that all submariners had to go through in order to become a member of the silent service; and of course due to the extreme danger of their operations.

One of these dangers was that of being trapped inside a sinking submarine in deep water. In response to this the navy exhaustively researched many possible ways for foundering submarine crews to escape from their would-be tomb.

Fortunately the Navy possessed a very effective underwater breathing apparatus called the Momsen Lung, developed by Charles Momsen, a well-known pioneer of underwater rescue equipment design.

The Momsen Lung was of simple construction, consisting of a small, rubber, air bladder that was 'charged' before its

Members of the crew were berthed in the aft battery compartment of the boat – in the crowded living conditions the men have made room for a game of cards. (National Archives)

use. Connected to the bladder was a pair of flexible rubber coil tubes that the sailor breathed through via a mouthpiece. The lung was strapped to the sailor's chest and for an added measure of safety a nose clip was provided to prevent any water entering the sailor's nose. In theory the lung could be worn at depths up to 150 feet, and still provide a reasonable chance of the sailor escaping safely.

During the War the branch of service with the greatest percentage of losses was the silent service; although some submarine crewmen did escape sinking boats with their lives, the vast majority of sunken submarines went down with all hands.

C: LOADING TORPEDOES

A dangerous but necessary job aboard all US submarines was the loading of a fresh supply of torpedoes, the task requiring the use of many highly skilled crewmen and no small amount of patience. When a submarine returned from a war patrol, the men on board were given a much-needed time of liberty at one of many designated US Navy 'RnR' centers. Before the next war patrol new supplies had to be loaded on to the boat, including torpedoes. Each submarine was assigned to a specific group, each group with its own sub-tender. For loading of torpedoes and other goods, the submarine pulled along side its tender and docked; the torpedoes were then hoisted aboard the submarine and gently lowered into the hold.

D: TORPEDO LAUNCH DIAGRAM

Although a smoke stack on the horizon could belie a possible target to an alert watchman, after 1942 submarines were most likely to make contact with a target using the surface search SJ radar. These radar would provide a good contact at eight to ten miles and were capable of making an intermittent reading at 20 miles. Despite their finicky nature and the difficulty of calibrating and reading them the radars gave the submarine an excellent advantage when hunting for a target.

In favorable weather the boat's skipper would use the information on bearing and speed provided by the radar to make a surface dash or 'end run' ahead of the target in order to set up a viable firing solution. Submerged the submarine would lie patiently in wait before firing.

Ideally the target would be on the submarine's beam. The submarine would be positioned in such a way as to form the apex of a right angle between the target's current position and predicted position (1). It would then start its approach. Using the periscope mounted ST radar the skipper would keep appraised of the target's course and bearing and calculate the angle on the bow, or relative bearing from target to sub if viewed from target (2).

All data thus far collected, line-of-sight range to target (3), speed and angle on the bow, would be fed into the Torpedo Data Computer (TDC) that automatically computed the optimum firing solution and adjusted the torpedo gyros accordingly.

Optimum firing range (4) was 1000 yards, with a zero degree gyro angle. The gyro angle was the angle through which the torpedo would have to turn after leaving the submarine to bring it onto a collision course with the target. The track angle or angle between the target's course and the torpedo's course (5) would be optimized at 100 degrees. The best firing solution having been achieved the torpedo tubes would be flooded and the 'fish' expelled by compressed air. The torpedo's course would be tracked by sonar and, is/was, until, hopefully, a hit was achieved.

E: MAKIN ISLAND RAID

In early August 1942 America had at last launched its first offensive of the Pacific when US Marines landed on the islands of Guadalcanal and Tulagi. The available resources for the operation were slender and any effort that could be made to delay the Japanese from reinforcing the garrison of the island needed to be considered. It was therefore determined that a raid launched against another Japanese-held island group might divert Japanese reinforcements from Guadalcanal as well as probe the state of Japanese defenses. The target chosen for the raid was Makin Island, a small atoll in the Gilbert Islands group approximately 2,000 miles southwest of Hawaii.

The task of taking the atoll was given to Colonel Evans F. Carlson and companies A and B of the Marine raider battalion under his command. This force was to be embarked aboard the navy's two largest submarines USS *Nautilus* SS-168 and USS *Argonaut* SS-166. Both of these vessels had been designed as 'cruiser' submarines armed with two 6-inch deck guns. The boats were stripped of all excess gear in order to make room for the company of Marines that they were to take aboard, including torpedoes being removed from both torpedo rooms and extra bunks being rigged for the raiders.

The small task force under Commander J.M. Haines set out on August 8, 1942 heading for the Gilbert Islands. Almost at once things began to go wrong – the air-conditioning unit that had been 'beefed-up' was insufficient to keep the vessels cool and conditions below decks soon became unbearable with temperatures rising well over 100 degrees. Additionally, many of the young raiders had difficulty gaining their sea legs and were miserable with seasickness. Haines, in order to alleviate the intolerable conditions below decks, allowed the skippers of both submarines to give the Marines ten minutes a day on deck in order to get some air and work off the edge of their confinement.

Both submarines arrived on station off Makin on the morning of August 16, 1942. Conditions for the landing were hardly ideal and high seas and rain hampered the efforts of the raiders to launch their motorized rubber boats. Many of the Johnson 6hp motors failed to function properly so Evans decided to abandon his initial plan of multiple landings and take the entire force ashore in one place, the non-motorized rafts being towed by the few that were functional. By 0513 reports arrived that the Marines had arrived on the beach.

However, as the Marine raiders struggled ashore from their small boats hampered by the high surf off the beach, the small Japanese garrison organized its resistance and brought them under heavy machine-gun and sniper fire. The garrison was on the alert looking for possible action having heard of the American landings on Guadalcanal that had occurred the day before.

Supplies being loaded aboard USS *Dace* SS-247 at New London submarine base prior to a training mission. Of note is the ship's bell positioned at the rear of the conning tower – it was standard to remove the bell before the boat when on patrol for safekeeping. (National Archives)

Meanwhile as the fierce fighting raged on the beaches and jungles of Makin Island Lieutenant Commander W.H. Brockman maneuvered *Nautilus* into a position where she could bring indirect fire from her 6-inch guns on the Japanese vessels at anchor in the lagoon. In spite of the poor visibility and the extreme range the *Nautilus* gunners were able to sink both of the Japanese ships.

At approximately 1130 Japanese aircraft appeared over Makin and both *Argonaut* and *Nautilus* were forced to dive – for the time being the Marines were entirely on their own. The raiders beat back two Banzai attacks during the course of the action that virtually wiped out the enemy garrison. Additionally, the Marines used their machine guns and anti-tank rifles to destroy two flying boats that had landed in the lagoon.

As night fell both submarines surfaced and made preparations to take the Marines back aboard. Difficulties with the outboard motors for the rubber rafts continued and on the first night only seven boats made it back to the submarines. Because several of the rescued Marines were wounded the wardrooms of both submarines were converted into operating rooms to aid the raiders.

By dawn the submarines had moved closer to the beach but a sudden air attack by the Japanese forced them under once again. In spite of possible air attack Commander Haines ordered both submarines to surface later in the morning and the weary raiders slowly made their way back to *Nautilus* and *Argonaut*.

By midnight all but 30 of the Marines were accounted for and the submarines set course for Pearl Harbor.

It was later discovered that nine of the raiders who had somehow become separated from the main body of Marines were captured and executed by beheading by their Japanese captors.

F: NIGHT ACTION

One aspect of the submarine service that was unique to the branch was the ability of the boat to engage in both surface and submerged action. Initially, American boats were fairly lightly armed with only a single deck gun that ranged in size from 3-inch to 5-inch. Anti-aircraft fire was provided by flexible-mount light-machine guns that were removed and replaced when the submarine submerged and surfaced.

As the War went on it soon became apparent that the anti-aircraft defense complement of weapons was grossly inadequate for the job of defending the boat from air attack. In order to increase the firepower of submarines the conning towers of boats were cut down to provide platforms for additional guns. At first these were 20mm Oerlikon cannons but later the weapons were upgraded to 40mm Bofors guns.

Surface actions were more common when it became known that the Japanese were operating their vessels with Sumatra crude oil, a highly flammable fuel. Whenever possible US boats would engage Japanese tankers with guns due to the explosive nature of this cargo.

G: LIFEGUARD DUTY

Although the primary mission of the silent service was to destroy Japan's supply lines, probably its most important role was the humanitarian mission of rescuing downed US aviators. With the 'Island Hopping' campaign in full swing, more and more dogfights were fought in the skies over the Pacific, and as with all battles there were casualties on both sides. When any large-scale air campaign was planned, a force of submarines was always called away from its commerce raiding duties to stand vigil as floating rescue bases for those unfortunate enough to be shot down. In close conjunction with seaplanes and other rescue craft, the submarines saved a huge amount of life – without them the fliers would be left to their own devices in the vast ocean.

Take the story of one Ensign George Bush, who one day in the summer of 1945 was flying a routine bombing mission over the tiny Japanese-held island of Chi-Chi Jima. His orders that day were to bomb a radio station. All went well until the Japanese returned fire and his Grumman TBF Avenger torpedo-bomber was severely damaged by flak. Ensign Bush managed to keep the aircraft in the air long enough for his crew to bail out before he himself attempted to jump out of his crippled plane. As Bush jumped out of the cockpit, he pulled his parachute cord too soon and hit his head on the tail of the aircraft; dazed but mostly unhurt Bush safely landed in the water.

USS *Finback* SS-230 was on patrol in the area of Bonin Island, of which Chi-Chi Jima was a part, picked up the young ensign and stowed him aboard for what would be a month-long stay aboard the boat.

H: HOMECOMING

The highlight of any member of the silent service's duty was finally returning to a home base; whether it was Pearl Harbor or Fremantle the long war patrol was at last over and the crews were due for some well-earned rest. At 'Pearl' the boats were greeted by brass bands and in this plate we see a Balao class boat ready to tie up alongside the pier. The ship's company has manned the sides and the war patrol pennants are flying from the boat's anti-fouling lines. Often the extreme wear and tear of a war patrol could be seen on the boat and the ship's company by the material damage to the boat and the extreme pallor of the crew.

Submarines were too small to warrant a regular chaplain as part of the crew – here an enlisted man conducts a church service aboard USS *Bullhead* SS-332 in the torpedo room for the crew. (US Navy Photograph)

INDEX

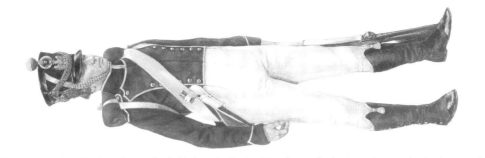 

OSPREY PUBLISHING

FIND OUT MORE ABOUT OSPREY

❏ Please send me the latest listing of Osprey's publications

❏ I would like to subscribe to Osprey's e-mail newsletter

Title / rank

Name

Address

City / county

Postcode / zip   state / country

e-mail

I am interested in:

❏ Ancient world
❏ Medieval world
❏ 16th century
❏ 17th century
❏ 18th century
❏ Napoleonic
❏ 19th century

❏ American Civil War
❏ World War 1
❏ World War 2
❏ Modern warfare
❏ Military aviation
❏ Naval warfare

Please send to:

USA & Canada:
Osprey Direct USA, c/o MBI Publishing, P.O. Box 1,
729 Prospect Avenue, Osceola, WI 54020

UK, Europe and rest of world:
Osprey Direct UK, P.O. Box 140, Wellingborough,
Northants, NN8 2FA, United Kingdom

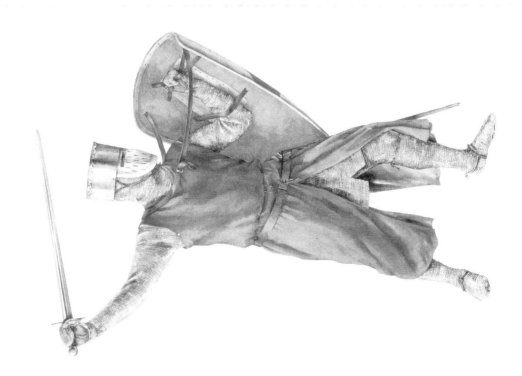

OSPREY
PUBLISHING

www.ospreypublishing.com

call our telephone hotline
for a free information pack

USA & Canada: 1-800-826-6600
UK, Europe and rest of world call:
+44 (0) 1933 443 863

Young Guardsman
Figure taken from *Warrior 22:
Imperial Guardsman 1799–1815*
Published by Osprey
Illustrated by Christa Hook

Knight, c.1190
Figure taken from *Warrior 1: Norman Knight 950 – 1204 AD*
Published by Osprey
Illustrated by Christa Hook

POSTCARD